RHYMING HISTORY

The Story of England in Verse

RHYMING HISTORY
The Story of England in Verse

by Colin Wakefield

Illustrations by John Partridge

VOLUME SIX: 1685 – 1688

James the Second, the Forgotten King

DHP
Double Honours Publications

RHYMING HISTORY
The Story of England in Verse

VOLUME SIX: 1685 – 1688
James the Second, the Forgotten King

First published in 2016 by Double Honours Publications.

ISBN 978-0-9570120-5-9

Double Honours Publications

Email: info@rhyminghistory.co.uk
Website: www.rhyminghistory.co.uk
Twitter: @Rhyming_History

Printed and bound by Short Run Press, Exeter

AUTHOR'S NOTE

This is Volume Six of our *Rhyming History* (still in the writing), which will eventually stretch from Julius Caesar's invasion of Britain in 55BC to the present day.

Volume Seven (The Glorious Revolution) will be published in 2017, with subsequent volumes appearing annually. All published volumes are available for sale through our website, Amazon Marketplace and selected retailers.

These books of verse are intended for those who want to learn more about our history, but in not too solemn a way. I hope they will also appeal to a wider audience, schools, students and historians, and those who simply enjoy reading verse.

Spellings from original sources have been modernised.

John Partridge has again provided witty and entertaining illustrations to accompany the text, for which I am as ever most grateful.

My special thanks are due to Jonathan Dowie for his detailed preparation of the text and for mastery of the website. I am also most grateful to Chris Moss for his help with the cover, to Alan Coveney for his expert advice on the text, to Janet Marsten and Roger Chamberlain for computer support and to Michael Callahan and Chris Wakefield for their continued help.

Please visit our website for updates on future volumes of the *History*, and for news of live performances of the verse.

www.rhyminghistory.co.uk

Colin Wakefield – February 2016

JAMES THE SECOND (1685 – 1688)

King James the Second. What can I say?   **1685**
The fool who threw his kingdom away.
He started well but, alackaday,
After four short years, in disarray,
He fled to France and called it a day.

A complex soul, it wasn't James' way
To compromise. To widespread dismay,
He sought to impose his will. Well, hey –
What use are subjects if not to obey?

Inheritance and character

James inherited from Charles, his brother,
A strong kingdom at peace, like no other.
For the last five years or so of Charles' life
A long episode of upset and strife
Had been brought to a close. The Popish Plot
(So-called) was a thing of the past. All rot,
Of course: it was pure invention, the lot.
The Exclusionists had been routed,
James' right to succeed no longer doubted.

In his latter years King Charles, at long last,
Indulged the Anglicans. They'd been aghast
At his lackadaisical attitude
Towards Catholics, and the latitude
He offered other dissenters. They feared
Creeping Catholicism. It appeared
That these anxieties were set to rest,
As Charles the Second did his level best
To reassure his apprehensive Church
He'd never, ever, leave them in the lurch.
Recusants were pursued, and the Test Acts
Rigorously enforced. These are the facts.

Rhyming History

Charles, the pragmatist, knew when to back down.
James (too tragic) was a fool and a clown.
Stubborn, unimaginative and dim,
He was rubbish at listening. To him,
Compromise equalled weakness. On this score,
King Charles the First had lost the Civil War
By failing to measure up to his foes.
Anyone with a glimmer of sense knows
That Charles' obduracy was his downfall.
He didn't seem to have the wherewithal
To heed an opposing thought. He'd stonewall.
He never saw the other side at all.

Where Charles the Second learned to duck and dive
(Unlike his father) – thus staying alive –
His brother James inherited, in spades,
Their father's intransigence. As young blades
They displayed similarities, of course.
Both were handsome, both looked good on a horse,
And both had an eye for the fairer sex
(That's an understatement). Both risked their necks
In battle, though too young by far to fight
In the Civil War; and neither was that bright.

Yet, from quite an early age, James needed
Order and structure. He best succeeded
When required to follow clear sets of rules.
It's said, as King, that he suffered no fools.
I take this as meaning (only my view)
That he hated surprise, anything new.
He enjoyed a brief, outstanding career
Under the great General Turenne. Here,
In the French army, were rules to obey,
Orders to follow. James liked it that way.
One of the major attractions, I'd say,
Of the Catholic Church (still to this day)

Is its disciplined structure, its ritual,
Its rites and strict sense of the spiritual –
Eagerly adopted as habitual
By the ever-devoted James. This passion
Caused his collapse in spectacular fashion.

Childhood

James enjoyed, as a young Duke of York should,
An apparently idyllic childhood.
This was to be rudely interrupted
By the Civil War. Life was disrupted
By the struggle between Parliament
And the King, his father. To what extent
A mere lad of eight would have understood
The political issues... No child could.

Yet I'm sure (at least, I strongly suspect)
That his *pater*'s plight had a keen effect
On wee James' character. Here's one sample –
A key event, a telling example.

By April 1642 the King
Was well aware of war in the offing.
Charles, on a whim, did a foolhardy thing,
Despatching his innocent son to Hull –
James could never complain that life was dull –
To secure the royal arsenal. He,
A boy, was sent to test the loyalty
Of Sir John Hotham, the town's Governor.
Young James soon found himself a prisoner.
For Sir John, no pushover, smelt a rat
And drew up the bridge, as simple as that.
When the King pitched up the following day,
He was told quite curtly to go away.
Courageous of Hotham? Dodgy, I'd say –
But Sir John refused entry, come what may.

This first salvo in the weapons race
Was won by the rebels. Charles lost face
And slunk away, as if in disgrace.
James was released. Hardly dramatic.
The long-term effect, though? Quite traumatic.

His dad's pitiful humiliation
Was not forgotten by James. The nation
Stood in peril. The Hull situation
Might have been better managed, the lad said,
By knocking Sir John squarely on the head.
For James was never one to 'wait and see'.
The 'direct approach' was his policy,
Winning hands down over diplomacy.
It just didn't work, unfortunately.

Civil War

Present at Edgehill, James was now aged nine.
Imagine anything more asinine
Than letting the first in line to the throne
(Charles) and his small brother wander alone
On the field of battle. They had, in fact,
A guardian – one however who lacked
Courage, common sense or concentration.
Dr. Harvey had a reputation
As a scientist. The circulation
Of the blood was the doc's discovery.
This hardly qualified him, patently,
To baby-sit a brace of young Princes.

A great cannon ball missed them by inches.
William Harvey woke up from his book
With a start. He didn't know where to look,
He was that embarrassed – I have to say
With all good reason. He led them away,
His precious charges, to a 'safer' spot.

There they encountered, believe it or not,
A stray contingent of the enemy.
Before they could be captured, luckily,
A royalist soldier saved the day:
A narrow escape, what more can I say?
The Princes both, without further delay,
Were taken to safety, off and away.
But the cut and thrust of arms… Imagine!
A taste of the war they were certain to win.

The thrill of battle for James (less so, perhaps,
For his brother, though both were impressive chaps)
Outlasted the Civil War. Throughout his life
He displayed a passion for warfare and strife.

Sadly for James, he enjoyed (this we shall see)
Only a limited opportunity
To pitch his talents against an enemy.
Yet, whatever James' failings, no one ever
Doubted his valour or his courage. Never.

Following Edgehill, James' war years were spent
At royalist headquarters. Heaven-sent!
For Oxford was simply the place to be –
A hive of martial activity.
But once the war was lost (by '46)
Poor James was in a pretty awful fix.
His dreadful mother had escaped to France.
She led her surly sons a merry dance,
Ever determined to convert the boys
To the Catholic faith. One of her ploys
Was to starve them of funds (once in exile),
Of food and affection. Vicious and vile.

By their father's express command, Charles, too,
Sought asylum in France. This, the King knew,
Was the surest option. Charles was his heir,
And as such could seek refuge anywhere
But at home in England. Folk wouldn't dare
(So the theory ran) depose their King
While his sons were at large. Sound reasoning –
Though this didn't stop them, in '49,
From chopping his head off. Cruel and malign.

Charles was safely abroad and James was... oops!
James was stuck in Oxford. As rebel troops
Closed in on the city, his time was up.
The Duke of York was a prisoner – yup!
Yet they showed him respect. I understand
That Oliver Cromwell offered his hand.
They gave him a tutor, treated him well
And put him up at a five-star hotel –

James the Second, the Forgotten King

St. James's Palace. Not being funny,
He wanted for nothing: pocket money,
Books, pets (they allowed his sister a dog).
Henry and Elizabeth played leap-frog
(For both were prisoners too), hide-and-seek…
But time still dragged: day on day, week on week,
Then months… two years almost. James was fourteen,
A brooding teenager, know what I mean?

He planned his escape. His efforts failed twice.
The third time, though, he was off in a trice –
Over the wall! Hide-and-seek was the key.
They'd waited so long, and so frequently,
On former occasions when James was 'he'
That they soon gave up and went off for tea,
Fully expecting him, nonchalantly,
To pitch up later. It wasn't to be.
James made his escape! To the Netherlands
He travelled, thence to France – into safe hands.

He was dressed as a girl, believe it or not.
You'd better believe it. It's part of the plot.

Exile

The next few years were frustrating indeed.
A life in exile's depressing – take heed.
James hadn't, alas, a great deal to do.
En route to Paris (I'm sure this is true),
He stayed some weeks, stopping over for free,
At a Benedictine monastery –
Saint Armand. Here he enjoyed his first taste
Of the Catholic creed. Far from shamefaced,
James lived with the monks for quite long enough
To relish his sojourn: all heady stuff.
Early days, but there's little room for doubt
That James in his youth was 'working things out'.

He'd finally reached Saint Germain-en-Laye
(His mother's 'Court'), when – oh, hideous day –
The news arrived they had long been dreading:
The King's murder. His wicked beheading
Had a lifelong influence (no surprise)
On his son, barely fifteen. Compromise
And lack of firmness had undone the King.
This was the lesson, above anything,
That James would take from his father's demise.
'Soft methods': deadly in the young Duke's eyes.
You'll witness this in the pages to come.
Where Charles gave ground, James would never succumb.

He rattled around, traipsing to and fro
From France to Jersey (where, I'll have you know,
The Duke served as Governor for a while);
Then to his elderly aunt, in exile
In Gelderland, the so-called 'Winter Queen' –
Elizabeth of Bohemia, seen
By many (though certainly not by me,
I'm a huge fan) as the epitome
Of Stuart misfortune. Sister Mary,

In the Hague, insisted on a visit.
Great to stay with family. But is it?
Only if you've nothing better to do.
This was the case with the Duke. Sad, but true.

He was thirsting for action. Charles had failed
At Worcester, his daring campaign derailed
To recover his throne. James kicked his heels,
Sick and frustrated, though never (one feels)
Faithless or ill-disposed to his brother.
Henrietta Maria (the mother)
Took comfort from Charles' extended absence
To seek to convert (it made perfect sense)
Her obstinate youngsters, James and Henry,
To the Catholic faith. As we shall see,
The former converted – though not for years.
As for poor Henry, it ended in tears.
Charles was cross. Let there be no talk of Rome.
Their mother was silenced. The boss was home.

Military success

Sadly, though, James still lived under her thumb.
He was mad for fame. This was far from dumb.
To seek glory in the cannon's mouth! Wow!
James came to prove himself worthy, and how!
Once free of Henrietta's apron strings,
He fought for France (of all unlikely things)
Against her neighbour, her enemy, Spain –
A lengthy, cumbersome, bloody campaign.

From 1652 to '55
The Duke won his spurs. His daring and his drive
Earned him a ferocious reputation.
His focus and his determination
Ensured a steady, impressive ascent
To unaccustomed heights. James was hell-bent

Rhyming History

On honour. A formidable fighter,
He learned all he knew (the lucky blighter)
From that great master of strategy, Turenne –
Legendary General and best of men.
Turenne pooh-poohed the hasty and dramatic:
His 'method' was ordered and systematic.
Ill-considered risks, the General averred,
Were wilful, wasteful, senseless and absurd.

Oh, that James had followed this prudent course –
His reign had been a triumph. A *tour de force*.
Alas, he displayed the wit of a horse
And in place of harmony courted divorce.

All that's for later. These were prosperous years
For James. He had no real choice of careers,
But the Army was perfect. Now aged eighteen,
He relished the discipline (this we have seen),
The day-to-day rigour, the welcome routine
Of military life. Heroic and bold,
He was loved by his fellows. Turenne, we're told,
Adored his recruit, who was willing to learn
And prepared to make war his living concern.

His commitment and courage earned him respect
And rapidly led (he was thrilled, I expect)
To his first commission, the coveted rank
Of Lieutenant-General. But James' heart sank
With lamentable news he received from France.
These tidings effectively scuppered all chance,
At a stroke, of Mazarin (French first minister)
Backing Charles Stuart. Equally sinister
Was the ease (nay, alacrity, truth to tell)
With which Mazarin, wooed by old Noll Cromwell,
Jumped into bed with the rogue. They agreed,
These hard-nosed bruisers, with indecent speed,
An anti-Spanish pact. Noll would provide
Experienced troops to fight side by side

With the French, in return (surprise, surprise)
For cash and (a far more strategic prize)
Dunkirk. Albeit in Spanish hands still,
This fortress, once taken (a bitter pill),
Guaranteed Cromwell command of the seas.

The Anglo-French agreement, if you please,
Contained a clause (a very cunning wheeze
On Oliver's part) requiring the French
To 'remove' the Stuarts. This was a wrench,
On a scale not that hard to imagine,
For James. It seemed that he just couldn't win.
He relished fighting for France. Mazarin
Would miss him sorely; Turenne, too. What's more,
Intrepid Irish soldiers, by the score,
Had enlisted with the French at James' behest,
Respectful of his reputation. At best,
They would desert in droves were the Duke to leave;
At worst, serve Spain. Mazarin sought James' reprieve.

In the service of Spain

It was brother Charles, though, who proved insistent.
The 'King' forced the pace. The Duke was resistant.
Charles had recently reached agreement with Spain
For her active assistance in his campaign
To recover his throne – completely in vain,
As it transpired. For sadly, time and again,
The Spanish failed him. They were far more concerned
With their own interests. By the time Charles learned
This manifest truth, though, his fingers were burned.

So James was forced to join the Spanish army,
In whose ranks he now fought (completely barmy)
Against his old mentor and master, Turenne.
Just how lunatic is that? Now and then
The glamour of warfare is stripped away,
Its madness made plain, I am glad to say.

I'm on my high horse. Be that as it may,
James displayed his usual gallantry,
Grit and courage in Spain's service. Sadly,
Her generals were of poor quality –
Unimaginative, vain and lazy.
Their strategy at times was plain crazy –
Witness the Battle of the Dunes. Cromwell
Had been promised Dunkirk. In a nutshell,
The Spanish were caught napping. Ill-advised
(Or blind, rather), they were faintly surprised
By the combined Anglo-French force mustered
To attack Dunkirk. A trifle flustered,
The Spanish determined, nevertheless,
To face down the enemy – sheer madness,
Given that Turenne was present that day
Commanding the French. Oh, and by the way,
Oliver's Ironsides had turned up too,
For England. The Spanish were sure to rue

Their choice of tactics. They hadn't a clue.
To turn on their heels was all they could do.

Ten days after the battle, sad to tell
(It's now 1658), Dunkirk fell.
James acquitted himself with great honour –
His brother Henry too. The full horror
Of warfare was made plain that sorry day
To the teenage Duke. The Prince of Condé
(Fighting for Spain, though French, I hope that's clear –
It's far more complex than it might appear)
Took Henry aside and asked him, straight out:
"Been in battle before?" There was no doubt
As to the Duke of Gloucester's honesty:
"No, sir," he replied. "Then soon you shall see
"One lost," opined the Prince, all too calmly –
"And in half an hour, approximately."

So it proved. As Spain went down to defeat,
Old Oliver Cromwell's joy was complete.
The Lord Protector, I'd say, was 'on song'.
This seasoned warrior could do no wrong,
Master of all he surveyed. Not for long!
Within four months of Dunkirk he was dead.
Gloom and despondency rapidly spread
Through royalist ranks. This has to be said.
Cromwell's demise, far from improving things,
Changed little. Isolated uprisings,
Sporadic and hopelessly organised,
Were quickly suppressed. No one was surprised
When the Stuarts in exile rapidly
Sank into their usual lethargy.

So James sought his fortunes further afield.
He was bored. A contract was all but sealed
For him to take command (yes, the top job)
Of the Spanish forces. Call me a snob,

But 'Lord High Admiral' was quite a gift.
It gave his gloomy mood a mighty lift:
Prize money, a huge salary, renown –
Fame and fortune! James couldn't turn it down.

The Restoration

Then, when they were all least expecting it,
The Protectorate crumbled, bit by bit.
Within months James was at his brother's side,
Bound for England, joyful and misty-eyed.

Restoration changed their lives for ever.
Nobody could claim that he was clever,
But James, Duke of York, had earned the respect
Of his peers. His hopes, though, were well-nigh wrecked
By one unfortunate indiscretion...

Anne Hyde

With James one does get the distinct impression
That women were a serious obsession.
Charles, of course, had mistresses by the score:
Duchesses, Ladies, even the odd whore –
Forgive me, I know you've heard this before.
Well, James followed in his footsteps. I've read
That he was a prize 'ogler'. Pepys, it's said,
Fretted himself over his wife's virtue
When the Duke was at large. Awful, but true.

In '56, when he was twenty-two,
James found himself attracted to Anne Hyde.
Some thought her plain, some on the pretty side.
She was most certainly witty, bright-eyed,
Though in middle life a little too 'wide',
If you catch my drift. Her eight pregnancies
Took their toll. Anne and James were chalk and cheese.
Where she was sharp and showed a ready wit,
James was slow. Where her charm was exquisite,
He suffered a charisma deficit.
And where he was handsome, dashing and tall,
Poor Anne, we're told, had no glamour at all.

Yet she and the Duke were not a bad match.
It goes without saying, James was a catch.
For Anne was a lowly maid of honour
To Mary of Orange. Well, good on her –
But hardly a prize qualification
For wife to Number Two in the nation.
Nevertheless, come the Restoration,
It emerged that James had made a contract
To marry the lass, accepted as fact
By the King himself, but broadly attacked
As a mismatch by James' chums and allies.

15

Rhyming History

What comes as rather a nasty surprise
Is that James tried to wriggle out of it.
Furthermore (another unpleasant bit),
When Anne fell pregnant and later gave birth,
The disingenuous Duke showed his worth
(Or lack of it, rather) by swithering.
The King, though, never one for dithering,
Took James firmly by the scuff of the neck
And made him see sense. James thought, "What the heck!",
Acknowledged his wife (and wee son, of course),
Packed off his mother (who'd yelled herself hoarse
In defiance of the match) back to France,
And offered Anne (big deal) a second chance.

Another figure who was furious
Was the Lord Chancellor. I'm curious
How the Earl of Clarendon (by the way,
He was Anne's pa, did I omit to say?)
Could have been so misguided and unkind
As to propose (was he out of his mind?)
That Anne should be despatched to the Tower
And her head chopped off within the hour.
The old Earl was fearful, simply no doubt,
Folk would suspect that he had used his clout
To encourage the romance between Anne
And James. Clarendon, so the rumour ran,
Fancied his chances as father-in-law
To the putative King James, and therefore
As grandfather to future royalty.
This didn't say much for his loyalty
To his present master, Charles the Second,
Unmarried, and generally reckoned
Pretty hopeless husband material.

If this sounds like a TV serial,
A royal 'soap', I should certainly say
It's not a bad story line. By the way,

Charles' future Queen bore him no progeny,
Which led the Earl's critics, cynically,
To hold him responsible. He, you see,
Had arranged the alliance. The irony
Is that Anne's issue did, eventually,
Succeed to the throne – Queens, both: first Mary
(With William), then Anne, but contrary
To any planning (of that I am sure)
On Clarendon's part. I know I'm a bore,
But no one could have anticipated –
Far less could the Earl have contemplated –
That both his granddaughters would become Queens.
How could he know? It wasn't in the genes.

I've no great wish to dwell on James' sex life –
Suffice to say, he cheated on his wife,
'Enjoying' scores of mistresses, we're told.
Although Anne Hyde was something of a scold
(Duchess of York, as now she was, of course),
James carried on regardless (what a sauce!) –

A greater lecher even than the King,
And that, believe you me, was quite a thing.
But where all Charles' mistresses were pretty,
Those chosen by James were at best witty,
At worst (as the King pointed out smugly)
Ordinary, coarse or just plain ugly.

Arabella Churchill and other mistresses

Charles once waggishly remarked that James' priests
Offered them as a penance – wicked beasts,
These elder brothers. His first proper love
(Anne apart: a mere wife, heavens above!)
Was Arabella Churchill – skin and bone,
Stick-tall, but with great legs (this was well known).
She was Anne's maid-in-waiting – *plus ça change*.
Though her flesh was as pale as cold blancmange,
James fell for the wench, hook, line and sinker.
Unfaithful he was, the little stinker,
Even to Arabella, but twelve years
She lasted. It ended, of course, in tears.

One of James' pages was her brother, John,
Who became (clearly the way to get on)
The Duke of Marlborough in later life,
The victor of Blenheim. Marlborough's wife,
Sarah Jennings, was 'close' (I'll say no more)
To Queen Anne. Sarah's influence, I'm sure
(Despite the rumours), was far from 'impure'…
Forgive me, I'm getting carried away,
For that's a story for another day.

The Duchess sadly died aged thirty-four –
Cancer, in those days no hope of a cure.
She bore eight children to the errant James.
Just two survived, Mary and Anne their names.

Her influence on James was quite profound.
She bossed him rotten, strange as that may sound.
When she converted to the Church of Rome,
She may have brought her new religion home.
For James about this time converted too:
The wife turns Papist – what else can you do?

This great development, I'm sure you know –
If not, you'll find it all explored below –
Dominated James' middle years, his reign
(Clumsy and brief) and his old age. The strain
Of reconciling Catholicism
(Or trying to) with Anglicanism
Gave rise to anger, mistrust and schism.
Add a pinch of stubborn optimism,
A dogmatic character (sad, but true)
And a wilful temperament and – phew! –
Quite a concoction. An explosive brew.

I'm running ahead. Arabella knew
That her time was up. Her looks on the wane
(Such as they were), she had little to gain
From pushing her luck. Twelve years. Not so bad.
La Churchill, however, was far from glad –
Abandoned, cross, disappointed and sad.

Catherine Sedley, ordinary, plain
And sensible, drove James fairly insane
With her unaffected, home-spun allure.
Yet mistress Sedley was shown the door
Upon James' succession. He tried, poor lamb,
To change his habits, but failed the exam.
His pious air was an absolute sham.
Though Catholic now, he cared not a damn
For personal, private morality.
Where Charles aroused hoots of hilarity

From his chums, and courted criticism
From his foes, the odd apt witticism
Put the latter sad spoilsports in their place:
Women and mistresses were no disgrace.
James' way was more tortured. He couldn't face
The shame of his adultery, his sin.
Yet nor could he give up his Catherine,
Soon back in his bed. His priests couldn't win.

Despite James' undoubted predilection
For women, the general complexion
Of his interests was (or so I've read)
Measured and sober. He kept a clear head
By abstaining from drink (preferring tea,
In a Duke a failing, it seems to me),
And never betting – though he loved racing,
A life-long pursuit he shared with the King,
And (fairly new) the sport of fox-hunting.

Lord High Admiral

The thrill of the chase (some say a dumb thing)
For an energetic Duke was one thing –
The lack of a good war was another.
Here James differed from the King, his brother.
He rared to have a pot-shot at the Dutch.
Shortage of funds didn't matter that much –
To James, at least. The Dutch were spoiling trade.
The Commons, indeed, were frankly dismayed
At the prospect of Dutch supremacy
In matters commercial. Put simply,
The Dutch threatened a trade monopoly.
James was by instinct a man of the sea.
He'd been Lord High Admiral (no, don't laugh)
From the tender age of four and a half.

The Duke took his duties seriously,
Devoting himself, assiduously,
To radical reform of the Navy –
The true bulwark of England's liberty.

In James' judgement it was just plain crazy
That her great fleet had been allowed to fall
Into disrepair – no money at all,
That was the big problem. The first Dutch War,
Fought to a win in 1654,
Was (in naval terms) England's finest hour.
But following Cromwell's death her sea power
Declined. Noll's successors, a dreadful shower –
Son Richard (ha!) and those who followed him –
Left the Navy to rot; signally dim.
Many sailors had gone unpaid for years,
Their wages (a scandal) in massive arrears.
Corruption was rife, money siphoned off,
Funding reduced to a spit and a cough.
Investment was down to a mere pittance.
Such was the Duke's sorry inheritance.

Yet James set about his task with a will.
Two of his cohorts are remembered still:
Sir William Coventry (a fine man)
And Sam Pepys, the diarist. So began
A well-organised and focused campaign
To knock the Navy into shape again.

James, though, was in too much of a hurry.
The King, his brother, was wont to worry;
Clarendon too was prone to hesitate,
Caution his watchword. But James couldn't wait.
The war faction, indeed, was in full cry:
The 1st Earl of Sandwich (destined to die
In the third Dutch War, in '72),
The Duke of Albemarle (George Monck to you)
And Sir William Penn – a noble crew.

Charles was bounced, assured by the war party
That England was ready. James was hearty
And far too confident. Pepys knew better.
Following instructions to the letter,
As a diligent civil servant should,
He feared (he was right) it would come to no good.

It was mainly a matter of supply.
Thousands of sailors were fated to die
Through the incompetence and vanity
Of James and his peers. Sheer insanity.
Sir William Coventry was aware,
As was Sam Pepys: the money wasn't there.

Victory at sea

James enjoyed early success nonetheless.
Victory off Lowestoft, I confess,
Gave rise to unreserved jubilation:
A well-deserved triumph for the nation.

Under James' command at least twenty-four
Fine ships of the Dutch were sunk, maybe more.
They suffered 8,000 casualties –
A conservative figure, if you please –
Burned, drowned or shot. It's numbers such as these
That cause us to pause a while and take stock.
The English dead alone were quite a shock –
Two hundred, we're told. Compared to the Dutch,
These few may seem not to matter that much.
But each and every victim was a son,
A husband or a father – every one.

James was fortunate to survive that day.
Enjoying, it appears, the fierce affray,
His pal, the Earl of Falmouth, was shot dead
At the Duke's very side. Richard Doyle's head,
Severed from his shoulders, flew through the air
And landed slap on the Duke (the King's heir),
Felling him to the deck. James was covered
With blood and brains, but quickly recovered.
We have Pepys to thank for this choice report
Of a battle bravely and keenly fought.

Retirement from action

The King, of course, was thoroughly dismayed
When the news reached him of this 'escapade'.
The possible risks were all too profound –
As policies go, distinctly unsound.
Should the Duke die in battle, the Crown Prince!
The third brother, Henry, had died long since,
Of smallpox sadly, in 1660 –
In the same outbreak, most tragically,
As James' own baby son. With Henry dead,
The Stuart royal line hung by a thread,
Dependent on James' girls, Mary and Anne,
Mere children. Now, the King was no great fan

Of his brother, considered him a fool,
A lightweight. But if James was born to rule,
Then rule he should. The King, as I live,
Was deaf to any alternative.

James was forbidden, after Lowestoft,
To hazard his life. Heartily browned off,
He withdrew from the front line. I don't know
(How could I? It was centuries ago)
Whether his 'exit' caused the sharp decline
In England's fortunes. One ominous sign
Was the Great Plague of 1665.
The Dutch seemed to slip into overdrive,
As English spirits could only nose-dive.

"The Dutch War," wrote Pepys, "goes on very ill."
Despite the Plague, the fleet was fighting still.
The Dutch too were fearsome adversaries:
Lowestoft was just first in a series.

In 1666 France joined the war –
On the Dutch side (I've no idea what for).
Charles was thus obliged to split his Navy,
Half against the French, the new enemy,
Half against the Dutch. Pepys was in despair.
"God knows," he noted (this seems not unfair),
"How little we are fit for it." In June –
The first of the month, shortly before noon –
Began the Four Days' Battle. I have read
That 5,000 English sailors lay dead,
And 2,000 Dutchmen, by the fifth day.
The English fleet (ten ships lost) limped away.
It was back in July. Crazy, I say.

All three parties were prepared to talk peace,
Eager, we're told, for the stalemate to cease.
Fate had other ideas. The Great Fire
Stopped Charles in his tracks. It doesn't require

A huge leap of the imagination
To understand how the conflagration
Weakened an already shattered nation.
London was burnt, broken, demoralised.
From the King down, nobody was surprised
That morale had reached rock bottom. The war
Trundled on. The country wasn't just poor,
But flat broke. The Lord Admiral, therefore
(With the backing of Sam Pepys, I suspect),
Made a choice that one can only respect.

The Dutch attack on the Medway

Hard as the decision was, James ordered
His ships to be brought to dock. This bordered
On insanity according to some.
But the Navy could barely afford rum,
Far less the manpower and guns needed
To wage war. The Duke's calls went unheeded
For fresh funds, though believe me he pleaded.
No surprise, then, that the Dutch succeeded

In their daring foray up the Medway.
Cool as you like, the Dutch fleet towed away
The *Royal Charles*, in the broad light of day,
Having torched a host of others: the *James*,
The *Royal Oake*... The English fleet in flames.

John Evelyn, never one for nonsense,
Wrote of "unaccountable negligence".
Another contemporary report
Spoke (with something of a derisive snort)
Of seven hundred and ninety-six men short –
Out of eight hundred on the naval pay-roll.
Economies may well have taken their toll,
But just four workmen on duty... Heads would roll.
Ammunition, too, had been a scarcity,
The powder poor to a critical degree:
"In all places" (this the epitome)
"The same face of supine security."

The Medway affair did the Duke no good.
That's no mystery. He did all he could
To cover himself. He declared ('touch wood')
That he'd always opposed the retirement
Of the fleet, a most galling requirement.
My firm belief (and I'm sticking to it)
Is that James didn't favour it one bit.
To limp home hurt simply wasn't his way –
His instinct, rather, was 'Anchors a-weigh!'
It's not that difficult to understand
How financial constraints forced his hand.

The outcome could well have been a lot worse.
The Dutch gave the English good cause to curse,
But were rapidly becoming weary
Of conflict. Merchants were far from cheery
At the prospect of their economy
In terminal decline. A collapse in trade
Made your average Dutchman very afraid.

The fall of Clarendon

The Treaty of Breda ended the war
On reasonable terms: a no-score draw.

New York remained ours (named after the Duke –
True), enabling us to cock a snook
At the Dutch. The King was slow to rebuke
His brother for any incompetence
He may have manifested in defence
Of the fleet. Less fortunate, however,
Was the Lord Chancellor. He had never,
Remember, supported the war. Who cared?
The knives were out, and he was only spared
By his well-timed flight to France. A fall-guy,
Clarendon (poor soul) had risen so high
That his fall was the more precipitous.

A scapegoat was called for. The impetus
Came from those such as Buckingham, the wretch –
A popinjay, wit and hideous lech –
And Castlemaine, the King's ageing mistress,
Who rejoiced in the sorry Earl's distress.

I'm grieved to report that the King, no less,
Joined the hue and cry – Charles, who owed his place,
His throne, to the Earl. A perfect disgrace.

James had better luck. At worst, he lost face.
Charles sent him (as Clarendon's son-in-law)
To urge the old man to resign before
He was pushed. The Duke was shown the door.
James nonetheless was one of the few at Court
Who stood by Clarendon. James was a good sport,
But laid himself wide open to attack.
As time went on he'd want to watch his back.
Subtle he was not. He hadn't the knack.

Naval service resumed

Five years later the Duke was back at sea.
1672, it seems to me,
Marked for James something of a turning point.

Thereafter life was ever out of joint.
Peace with the Dutch was never built to last.
The fragile trust disintegrated fast,
As Charles (Louis of France his new best friend)
Launched the third Dutch War. Where would it all end?

In a mess, is the blunt answer to that.
A naval round of bitter tit-for-tat
Led to no glorious triumphs – but hey,
What did you expect? That's war. Southwold Bay
Was one such clumsy encounter. The day
Belonged to nobody. The subtle Dutch
Saw off the English. That's not saying much.
James' uninspiring leadership was such
As to attract comment. Not once, but twice
He was forced to jump ship. That was the price
Paid for French knavery. Our sworn allies
Barely engaged at all. There's a surprise!

The Treaty of Westminster

1674 saw a new peace.
Parliament (wonders will never cease)
Balked at pouring good money after bad.
The King agreed the best terms to be had.

The Treaty of Westminster concluded
A long, draining conflict. I alluded
To James' return to the nautical fray.
He was now *persona non grata*. Hey,
I urge you not to get carried away.
But the Duke, it appears, had had his day.

Catholicism

I'd best explain. We shall have to go back.
James was effectively given the sack
In '73. It came down, of course,
To religion. Rome had been a force
In James' conscience now for several years.
His conversion (when it came) stoked the fears
Of all good Anglicans (like it or not)
Who feared, to their marrow, a Popish Plot.

By the late '60s, I'd hazard a guess,
James' mind was made up. I have to confess
That most authorities are uncertain
As to the date of the Duke's conversion.
The process was gradual. But once 'home' –
By which I mean in the bosom of Rome –
He was home for good. His entire life
Was transformed. It's possible that his wife
Exerted some influence. True or not,
James followed his conscience and fast forgot
King Charles his father's exhortation never
To abandon the Protestant faith, ever.

Politically it was far from clever
To break with the Anglican Church. However,
The more his brother took care not to sever
His Anglican links, the more the Duke set his course
Towards Rome and the Pope: no regrets, no remorse.

The Protestant majority in the nation
Saw Catholicism as an aberration.
The background to this hatred has been well rehearsed.
Prejudices ran deep. The Catholics were cursed.
Queen 'bloody' Mary definitely did her bit
To queer their pitch. Protestants had a purple fit
At the prospect of a Catholic Queen or King –
The stuff of nightmares. Yet this was the very thing

Threatened in 'King' James. For Charles had no heir, you see.
The Queen was barren. The ghastly reality
Of a Catholic sovereign had rapidly
Become more than a distant possibility.

Before long, James declared his faith quite openly.
It's been claimed that the King himself, clandestinely,
Was a Papist. It's true that Charles showed sympathy
Towards Catholics. When first he came to the throne,
One of his early guarantees (this is well known)
Was "liberty to tender consciences". Now,
Parliament soon put Charles in his place, and how!
But the King was ever one for toleration.
He could never comprehend the fascination

With force-feeding one man's honest-held religion
Down another man's throat. Simply not his pigeon.
Charles owed the success of his 'respectable' reign
(Twenty-five years, post-Restoration), in the main,
To his innate ability to duck and dive.
He understood instinctively how to survive.

This most relaxed and easy of Kings
Proposed, of all impractical things,
A Declaration of Indulgence.
This made, to Charles, the most perfect sense:
Broad toleration for dissidents –
Including Catholics. They'd be free
To worship in their own homes. To me,
This most fundamental liberty
Seems wise and just. It wasn't to be.
The measure provoked hostility
On a grand scale. Open popery
Was the great fear. Politically,
Charles had widely overstepped the mark.
Parliament's bite (worse than its bark
On this occasion) was keenly felt.
Already obliged to tighten his belt
In his need for funds for the third Dutch War,
Charles, to his chagrin, was forced to withdraw.

The Treaty of Dover

Now this I should have mentioned before.
Two years earlier (1670),
In a pact with France, the Dover Treaty,
The King had signed up in great secrecy
To a covert vow to convert, with speed,
To the Church of Rome! Why Charles felt the need
For such a pledge remains a mystery –
A great question mark of history.
Should the secret clause ever have leaked out,
It would have been curtains, simply no doubt.

His conduct was neither honest nor wise.
He told a catalogue of whopping lies
To Parliament: they'd nothing to fear;
The Dover Treaty was open and clear;
No clauses (one wonders how the King dared)
Bar those put out and already declared!

Why did Charles promise to turn Catholic?
It's often hard to know what made him tick,
But this! Utter madness! Was it money?
Louis the Fourteenth (this isn't funny)
Paid generous subsidies to the King
Under the Treaty. The important thing,
From his point of view, was to keep Charles sweet
When it came to the Dutch. Crafty, but neat.
English Protestants, given half the chance,
Would have sided with Holland against France.

Louis' treatment of the poor Huguenots
(French Protestants) was, as tyranny goes,
An outrage. Keeping cousin Charles on side
Was key. But was the latter (you decide)
Playing a canny game of double bluff?
His papist pledge was dangerous enough,
But was he serious? Nobody knows.
Yet James got most excited! I suppose
This was his dream. What soon got up his nose,
Though, was that Charles not only dragged his heels,
But changed tack. Now, bad faith never appeals,
But the King, in my humble submission,
Had no need of his brother's permission
With regard to changing his religion.

Neither James nor Louis was enamoured
Of the King. While Parliament clamoured
For him to drop his new Declaration,
Charles looked to the effect on the nation

Of sticking to his guns. Not to give way
Would cause, at best, significant delay
In fighting (and funding) the new Dutch War.
The Declaration had to go, therefore –
A U-turn we'd call it today, I think.
More quickly than most other monarchs blink
Did Charles, the great survivor, 'tack' and 'trim'.
Subtle and smart, I say – and good for him.

Now, here's the telling contrast. Brother Jim
(Or 'Dismal Jimmy', Nell Gwynne's *soubriquet*)
Would have fought tooth and nail, such was his way,
To save the Indulgence. Parliament?
Pah! The King proved a sore disappointment.
Weak or what? You had to show who was boss.
You could hardly get your message across
By caving in. Fair to say, James was cross.
He still remained loyal to Charles, but hey –
He'd show 'em all when he was King one day.

Resignation as Lord High Admiral

Not only was the Declaration dropped,
But Charles' authority was further 'cropped'
By Parliament, in '73,
With a Test Act. The measure was petty,
Vindictive and quite unnecessary.
Its intent and effect were, patently,
To exclude all Catholics from office.
Targeted at the Duke, it couldn't miss.
Office holders were obliged, for their sins,
To denounce certain Catholic doctrines.
Charles gave his royal assent to the Bill,
Which denied his brother (a bitter pill)
The right to serve. James was forced to resign
As Lord High Admiral. He drew the line

At taking the Test. Thomas Clifford, too,
(Of the Cabal) refused. Well, wouldn't you,
Were you a Catholic? There are far too few
Who cherish their beliefs (my personal view).
Dismissal, to Clifford, cut like a knife.
He resigned, retired, then took his own life.

James, of course, lived to fight another day.
He stepped down, yes, but it wasn't his way
To bow to his critics. And, come what may,
Was he the King's brother or wasn't he?
He was heir apparent, couldn't they see?
Deny him his right? It wasn't to be.

It very nearly was, in point of fact –
Not as a direct result of the Act,
But through political pressure. James lacked
Imagination, prescience and tact.
Neither the Duke nor (fair to say) the King
Foresaw the disaster that was brewing.

One obvious effect of the Test Act
Was to blow his cover. To be exact,
James' Catholicism was now patent –
Or, in the eyes of the cynics, blatant.
Not that the arrogant Duke cared a hoot.
His faith, he believed, was his strongest suit.
Most Englishmen of honour, anyway,
Were Catholics at heart and, come the day
When a papist monarch sat on the throne,
England at last would come into her own.

Second marriage

This view, at very best, was rarefied.
Most English Protestants were terrified.
Their fears were hardly alleviated
By James' second marriage, celebrated

James the Second, the Forgotten King

Three years after the death of his wife Anne.
Within months of her demise there began
(With indecent haste, it has to be said:
James cared not a fig that his spouse was dead)
The hunt for her successor. Charles insisted
On royal blood. Sadly, there existed
A shortage of suitable candidates.

Mary of Modena

In those days princes didn't go on dates.
No, ambassadors were despatched abroad
To scour the foreign courts, while at home, bored,
The putative husband would sit and wait.

A portrait might be produced. Thirty-eight?
Too old. Thirteen? Too young – at any rate
For a lecherous Duke pushing forty.
Finally (and this was fairly naughty,
Given their respective ages) the choice
Fell on Mary of Modena. She'd no voice,
In that nobody heeded her, no one.
Indeed, she'd been set on becoming a nun.

At fifteen, however, and fair of face,
Sheltered (she'd never heard of such a place
As England), pure in heart and full of grace,
The Princess was perfect. What made folk sick
Was that James' young wife was a Catholic.
Deeply unpopular, "the Pope's daughter"
They called her, poor girl. That should have taught her!

It didn't. Mary was a loyal wife
To James and throughout his turbulent life
Stood by him with honour and decency –
A tower of strength, as soon we shall see.

These were most fretful and frustrating years
For Charles' younger brother. Protestant fears
Of a Catholic succession grew.
The Queen was childless. Everyone knew
That even in the event of the King
Predeceasing James the most likely thing
Was for Mary (or Anne) in time to succeed.

What now, though, should Mary of Modena breed?
For James, by marrying his teenage Princess,
Had raised the stakes. It wasn't mere carelessness,
His critics opined, but naked policy.
His daughters, the aforesaid Anne and Mary,
Were staunch Protestants. The King had seen to that.
But should James now have a son, I'll eat my hat
Were the child to be taught any other truth
But that of the Church of Rome and the Pope. Strewth!
Quite a conundrum, and one that terrified
The host of Protestant zealots countrywide.

James found himself increasingly vilified.
Folk sought desperate ways to sideline the Duke.
One suggestion (which earned a stern rebuke

From the King) was that Charles should divorce his wife,
The good Queen Catherine, and start a new life
(The nerve) with a consort rather more fertile.
Charles abhorred the idea: hardly his style.
The most appalling proposal by a mile
Was that Catherine should be put on a boat
Bound for the Americas. Sorry to gloat,
But this was Buckingham's absurd contribution,
Rejected by Charles as a third-rate solution.

'Exclusion'?

Indeed, the King saw no problem at all.
'Exclude' the Duke? He refused to play ball.
Legitimise Monmouth, his eldest son?
A non-starter. He'd had his fair share of fun
With Lucy Walter, the wanton mother.
But to disinherit his kid brother
In favour of their bastard progeny?
The thin end of the wedge, quite honestly.

Monmouth himself (he was trouble in store;
He took arms against James, need I say more?)
Even made claim he was legitimate.
A 'Black Box' (though nobody could find it)
Contained all the papers, absolute proof
Of a marriage! The King hit the roof,
Published a denial (well, wouldn't you?) –
But rumour was rife. He could hardly sue,
And when push came to shove, what could he do?

The Lucy Walter saga rumbled on
Long after Charles was forgotten and gone.
It haunted King James. It has to be said
That only when Monmouth had lost his head
Did 'Dismal Jimmy' sleep safe in his bed.

Princess Mary and William of Orange

In '77 the King agreed
To an Anglo-Dutch marriage. The need
To humour his Protestant subjects was,
To put it mildly, pressing – this because
His pro-French foreign policy gave rise,
At home, to forebodings (surprise, surprise)
Of despotism and absolute rule.
King Charles the Second was nobody's fool.
His first minister, Danby, was pro-Dutch,
Ever wary of the French and, as such,
Urged Charles to give his blessing to a match
Between his young niece Mary (quite a catch)
And William of Orange (his nephew).
For Danby this was something of a *coup*.
It offered, at last, a notable chance
To tweak the nose of King Louis of France.

It may seem odd, but Charles wasn't averse.
He was watching his back. He could do worse
Than to offer avuncular support
For this Protestant union. He sought,
Thereby, to reassure Parliament
Of his pro-Dutch tendencies. He was bent,
Also, on prompting Will to sue for peace
With his French neighbour. Louis might release
(Ha!) his grip on the Spanish Netherlands,
Which William (or so one understands)
Was all too keen for the French King to do.
The Dutch Prince was far from naïve. He knew
That Louis was unlikely to withdraw.
He planned (unlike Charles) to step up the war,
Once the King was his new uncle-in-law.

As for Mary, no one asked her of course.
This was politics. Charles felt no remorse

James the Second, the Forgotten King

In offering his niece (not very nice)
As a cheap political sacrifice.
A sensitive child and barely fifteen,
Mary was thrown to the wolves. It's obscene.
Her husband was twelve years her senior, Dutch
And a hunchback. Need that have mattered so much?
To his wife? I should say! Whatever your views,
It's awful they didn't allow her to choose.
He was four inches shorter – terrible news
In an age (I'm assured) before platform shoes.
William was serious, hardly a laugh;
His wife-to-be cried for a day and a half
When informed of her fate. I'm glad to report
That her fears (and his foibles) counted for naught.
No marriage is perfect, Heavens above –
But theirs was a model of friendship and love.

What of our pal, the Duke? What was James' view,
As Mary's papa? If only we knew!
He wasn't consulted. He had no say.
Charles gave his consent, but brooked no delay,
Disregarding his brother. To this day
It's a moot point. "The King shall be obeyed,"
They quote James as saying. He felt betrayed
(My own surmise), disgruntled and dismayed.

His discontent wasn't unqualified.
By remaining supportive, dignified
And outwardly submissive, the Duke hoped
To recover some credit. How he coped
In private we can only imagine.
Yet, by appearing to hold it no sin
For Mary to marry a Protestant,
James hoped that folk would become less distant,
Less nervous, less hostile… less resistant
To his belonging to the Church of Rome.
Unpopularity was hitting home.

But far from famine giving way to feast,
Sadly the animosity increased.
Public opinion's a fickle beast.

November the 4th was the wedding day.
The sky was heavy, overcast and grey.

Will was dry and reserved; Mary, tearful;
Princess Anne was absent (they were fearful
For her life: she had smallpox); the Duchess
(The stepmother) occasioned some sadness
By her non-attendance. She was pregnant.
A boy? The idea was repugnant.
Such thoughts lay heavy on every mind
That fateful day. No wish to be unkind,

But William was praying fit to bust
For a female child. If give birth she must,
Let Mary of Modena bear no son
To disinherit his wife. The deed done
(The nuptials), it was left to the King
To lift their spirits. He set to toasting,
Merriment, jokes and all-round back-slapping –
In an uncle faintly embarrassing.
Poor William. Charles urged him (with a smirk)
To his 'duties': "Hey, nephew, to your work!
"St. George for England!" It's not reported
How (or whether) young Orange retorted.

The Duke behaved well, to give him his due.
For a while relations between the two
(William and James) were cordial. Phew!
I hate these family fall-outs, don't you?

But over the next eight years this accord
Grew stale. Arrogance reaps its own reward.
Not only did James seek to patronise
His son-in-law (decidedly unwise),
But contrived in time to antagonise
This fine Dutchman. It comes as no surprise –
When England seemed ready to fall apart
Under King James and needed a fresh start –
That they called for William. This was smart.

The Popish Plot

All that's for later. I'm running ahead.
Our interest should be focused instead
On that scary event, the Popish Plot.
James was almost undone, like it or not,
By whispers and rumours, the blind panic
That swept the land. The mood was satanic,
Hazardous, venomous, mean and manic.

Rhyming History

Catholics were planning the overthrow
(Allegedly) of the King. You should know
That his death, in the most minute detail,
Was carefully plotted. It couldn't fail.
Charles was to be shot. Should this plan misfire,
The conspirators aimed (sorry) one higher:
Murder by poison – a certain success,
Served up by the King's physician, no less.
Should poison miscarry, stabbing (it's said)
Was next on the list. The books that I've read
Suggest that the foul killing of the King
Would herald a Catholic uprising.
Finally, France (it's hardly surprising)
Invades. Ireland rebels. From Rome, the Pope
Arrives with his train. I ask you, what hope
Did a plot of such wild fabrication
Have of seizing the imagination
Of a decent, if credulous, nation?

The Popish Plot was preposterous, yet
England was ready for fireworks – you bet.
Anti-Catholic prejudice ran deep.
Protestant bigots, like so many sheep,
Were led to believe (were they half-asleep?)
That the Pope, the Irish, the King of France,
Were engaged in some sick, demonic dance.
Since 'bloody' Mary's despicable reign,
The threat from the Papists was all too plain.
These dreadful conspirators did their worst
With the execution of Charles the First.
Who started the Fire of '66?
All too obvious: papist fanatics!
The Pope in Rome was openly cursed.
England was furious, fit to burst.

How could Protestants have been quite so dumb?
They were primed pitch-perfect, ripe to succumb.

Yet Israel Tonge and Titus, his chum,
Had luck on their side nonetheless – then some!

Titus Oates

Titus Oates was a hapless, hopeless man:
A liar, a loafer, an also-ran.
He finished nothing he ever began.
Expelled from countless universities,
Schools and colleges, here and overseas –
Many of them Catholic, if you please –
He brought the country nearly to its knees.
Dishonesty was Titus' middle name,
Plotting and subterfuge his claim to fame.
He and Tonge reckoned (cynical or what?)
That by framing the odd, grisly plot,
And naming names, they could whip up the mob,
Destroy the odd life and make a few bob.

In short, it started as a bit of fun.
The outcome, though, in terms of damage done,
Took both these rogues entirely by surprise.
The fire raged on before their very eyes.
When first the King was made aware of it,
We're told that he exploded in a fit –
Of laughter! He gave the tale no credit,
None at all, not the slightest little bit.
The plot was riddled with absurdity:
Let others listen to the birds, not he.

I suspect you may be wanting a date:
This was August 1678.
Danby decided to investigate.
The Duke expressed an interest as well –
Precisely why, it's difficult to tell.
Perhaps he understood the latent risk
Of feigning nonchalance. Best to be brisk,

Detach himself from the Catholic cause
(On this occasion) and command applause
By openly acknowledging the charge:
There could be wicked Catholics at large.

Edward Coleman

Alas, the strategy badly misfired.
A rabid Papist whom James much admired –
One Edward Coleman, his secretary,
A passionate convert to popery –
Was fingered by Oates as a key plotter.
Coleman (the sleaze) was an outright rotter.
His correspondence was seized (all in code),
Which proved that he'd trodden the well-worn road
Of treason. Letters he wrote, by the score,
To Rome, full of fantasies, hopes galore:
Once Charles the Second was shown the door,
Our James would be King! Salvation in store!
Conversion for England beckoned – and more.

Coleman received a tip-off from a friend
To burn his letters. It was a godsend
To Titus that he ignored this advice.
Ed was arrested (it's not at all nice),
Tried, sentenced, beheaded – all in a trice.
His guilt had nothing to do with the 'Plot' –
For none existed! It was so much rot!
But Coleman, alas, deserved all he got.
It's fair to say that the wheels of justice
Spun fast in his case. Why so? Simply this:
Whether James was aware, or whether not,
His assistant's treachery was a blot,
A deadly stain, on his private honour.

Once assured that Coleman was a goner,
The Duke of York could sleep safe in his bed –
A feeble excuse, it has to be said,

44

For the execution of a traitor,
Guilty though he was. We shall see later
How James bounced back from this closest of shaves.

It's telling that Oates (the shrewdest of knaves)
Never personally accused the Duke.
He earned himself a withering rebuke,
From Charles, when he sought to involve the Queen.
A plot to murder her husband… I mean!
James was happy to keep his own nose clean
As Coleman was left to his fate. Obscene.

The murder of Sir Edmund Berry Godfrey

For Oates, one further fortunate event
To fuel the Protestant discontent
Was the gruesome murder of the JP
Who'd heard his deposition. Now, to me,

Rhyming History

It does appear singularly unlikely
That Sir Edmund Berry Godfrey – whose body
Was the object of a grim discovery
On Primrose Hill – committed suicide.
This far-fetched theory (though you decide)
Stemmed from the fact Godfrey had been run through
With his own sword. But he'd been strangled too!
I should have thought (of course, only my view)
This might have been a tricky thing to do –
To strangle himself with a rope, then stroll
To Primrose Hill, with perfect self-control,
And stab his own dead body with his sword.

I hear you chorusing with one accord:
"A likely story!" Godfrey's shoes were clean,
Which also begs the question where he'd been.
Not out for a walk, that's perfectly clear,
For the ground was muddy and wet. Oh, dear –
We're floundering rather. Robbery, then?
Now that's far more likely. Ten out of ten.
Yet… Sir Edmund still had money on him.
What kind of footpad would kill, on a whim
(A hanging offence), then forget the cash?
Not only dim, but decidedly rash.

The more I consider it, suicide
Does seem possible. I'm not qualified
To judge, but his kinsmen may have sought ways
To cover up his offence. In those days
Self-murder was a crime, a most dreadful shame.
To avoid disgrace to the family name
And to save his estate from forfeiture –
Not just his house, fittings and furniture,
But the sum total of Sir Edmund's wealth –
He couldn't be seen to have hanged himself.
His brother, then (so the theory goes),
Cut him down and, one can only suppose,
Bore his body to Primrose Hill. Who knows?

The stabbing was perhaps an afterthought.
Who cared if the wrong 'assassins' got caught?

The unexplained death of Berry Godfrey
Remains a tantalizing mystery.
Not so, though, in 1678:
His 'killing' was seen to substantiate
The entire premise of the Popish Plot –
A vile conspiracy. It had the lot:
A corpse; a magistrate; an enigma;
The awesome death of the very figure
To whom Oates had sworn his deposition
And a friend (for such was the position)
Of the aforementioned Coleman, no less.
A scandal indeed, I have to confess.
For Godfrey, it seems, had Catholic links,
Though Protestant himself. Frankly, it stinks.
Mark this: Sir Edmund was the self-same chum
Who tipped Coleman off. Coincidence? Come!
Murky waters… Chaos and confusion…

Folk at large, whether from self-delusion
Or sheer prejudice, reached one conclusion:
Godfrey had been slain by the Catholics
To shut him up. Cue: public hysterics.

Panic gripped the capital. Fine ladies
Carried pistols under their capes; rabies
Infected Papists (I made that bit up);
Poison laced every communion cup;
The French were said to have landed at night
(The Spanish, too) to set London alight;
The prisons were full to overflowing
With Catholic priests. There was no knowing
Where it would end. To celebrate Berry,
Commemorative daggers were sold. He,
This quiet and unassuming JP,

Became a martyr. *Memento Godfrey*
Was carved on these weapons. Anybody
With a grudge could stand up and cry "Guilty!"
At a blameless man. Nobody dared, see,
Gainsay their guilt. Remember McCarthy?
The Salem 'witches'? Three men (innocent)
Died for Godfrey's murder. Parliament
Played its part in the farce. All Catholics
Were barred from sitting. You see how mud sticks?
The House of Lords was purged of papist peers –
The Duke of York excepted, it appears.

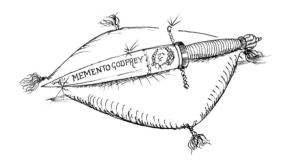

As time wore on, even to doubt the Plot
Was evidence of guilt. Like it or not,
Oates was a lucky chap. Sir Edmund's death
Corroborated his every breath,
His every last rancid, rotten word.
Titus was the toast of London. Absurd.

The King, as ever, steered a middle course.
As manic Protestants yelled themselves hoarse,
Charles poured scorn on Shaftesbury's calls to bar
James from the succession. One bridge too far.
But, for reasons not hard to understand,
He agreed (on the one hand) to disband
His standing army and (on the other)
To clip the wings of his younger brother.

James was barred from various committees –
Many regarding matters overseas –
And the Admiralty Board, if you please.
Charles also agreed (this a cunning wheeze)
To enforce the long-standing penalties
Against Catholics with greater rigour.
Cynical, I know. Well you might snigger.
But this bold show of Protestant vigour
In due course did the King no harm at all.
The gale-force winds he quelled to a mere squall.

James despatched abroad

The greater the panic generated
By the Plot, the more Charles contemplated
The future of his Catholic brother.
James was a stubborn ass like no other.
The Archbishop of Canterbury,
William Sancroft, and George Morley,
The Bishop of Winchester, urged the Duke
To quit the Church of Rome, to cock a snook
At the Pope and to return (oh, brother!)
"To the bosom of your holy mother,
"The Church of England". James refused, point blank.

For saving his skin he had Charles to thank.
The Duke's default mode was confrontation.
The King knew better. The more the nation
Smouldered with anti-papist discontent,
The more Charles sought a cooler way. He sent
(Mark this) the Duke of York abroad, post-haste.
Anger and fireworks were not to his taste.

James' honour was now seriously soiled
By Coleman's guilt. He was deeply embroiled
In the crisis (at one remove, it's true)
By references in Coleman's letters to

"The salvation of his soul" – James', that is –
And "the conversion of our kingdom". This,
Take note, was political dynamite.
James was fortunate that his 'acolyte',
His *quondam* secretary, died the death
Of a loyal friend, uttering no breath,
Not a word, against his master, the Duke.
Lucky, very. It may have been a fluke,
But James, albeit dogged by suspicion,
Retained his precarious position
(Perilous indeed) as heir to the throne.
He owed this to Charles and to him alone.

Charles stands up to the Exclusionists

James was despatched to Brussels. This was now
March '79. James was bored, and how!
His absence saved his bacon, though, I vow.
Charles (and good for him) refused to kowtow
To the Exclusionists – known as 'Whigs'.
In late May the House of Commons, the pigs,
Approved a Bill barring James from the throne –
By almost two to one, that much is known.

With James no longer breathing down his neck,
The King enjoyed a free hand. A rain check:
Why confront the Commons? Why cause a stink?
Charles held all the cards. So, what do you think?
He prorogued, then dissolved, Parliament.
Just like that! Dissolution, of course, meant
That the first Exclusion Bill (so-called) lapsed.
For now, the move against the Duke collapsed.

The King was stronger than it might appear.
Cave in to toads like Shaftesbury? No fear!
Charles had more ready cash than in the past.
His domestic income had, at long last,

Increased, thanks largely to chaps like Danby;
Subs from France were still coming in handy;
And he'd even managed to make savings
At Court, despite his mistresses' cravings.
Happily he was far less reliant
On the wiles and whims of Parliament.
The King was becoming independent.

Charles had another edge over the Whigs.
None of the exclusionist bigwigs
Could agree on a substitute for James.
Monmouth was mooted as one of the names,
The King's bastard son. Completely absurd.
Then there was Mary. You can take my word:
Although she was Protestant, folk weren't keen.
Apart from being a mere seventeen –
Too young by far for a putative Queen –
Her husband was foreign (know what I mean?).
Will was a warmonger, Dutch and, far worse,
A Stuart (well, half…). It may sound perverse,
But the years that followed of James-baiting,
Exclusion attempts and Papist-hating,
Led honest men (when it came to a King)
To wonder if James was such a bad thing.
Ironic, absurd – and astonishing.

The King falls ill

Indeed, within six months of his exile
James was recalled. The King (hardly his style)
Fell sick. They feared the worst. Those who'd advised
Charles against his brother soon realised,
With horror, the awful consequences
Of 'King' Monmouth (not least, Charles' mistresses).
The crisis brought them fast to their senses.
The terrible prospect of Civil War
United the Court as never before.

James hurried home, hailed as a saviour.
His critics (sickening behaviour –
Shaftesbury and Halifax excepted)
Grovelled (not entirely unexpected)
And kneeled before him. James was a shoe-in!
The Earl of Sunderland came a-wooing,
Fawning on him, flattering and cooing.
The Earl was to be the fool's undoing,
An early cause of his royal ruin…
But that's for later. London's Lord Mayor
Kissed James' hand and said a little prayer.
Who'd have dreamt it, just half a year before?
Artful, I call it. I'm shocked to the core.
Two-faced and shallow, they all knew the score:
James had to succeed, according to law.

Charles rapidly rallied. Embarrassing?
Perhaps. But for now the King was still King.
The Whigs had their fingers severely burned.
Some interesting lessons had been learned.

The defeat of Shaftesbury

Shaftesbury for one was gravely concerned.
His 'disciples' were increasingly spurned.
Although James, upon Charles' recovery,
Was sent packing again, the Whig 'party'
(As it effectively became) lost ground.
Charles knew what he was doing, I'll be bound.
With a new Parliament elected,
The Commons (this was to be expected)
Voted afresh to bar the Duke of York
From the succession. Was it all talk?
Certainly not. In the Lords, Shaftesbury
Battled it out with Halifax. Sadly
(For the Exclusionists), Halifax
Won the day. Could Charles begin to relax?
I'll say! When he suffered renewed attacks,

This Parliament he also dissolved,
Its two successors to boot. Problem solved.

Shaftesbury's star was now well on the wane.
The daft doodle tried again and again
To prove Monmouth's true legitimacy.
He refused to give up lightly, you see.
Charles nicknamed him 'Little Sincerity' –
Most singularly apt, it seems to me.
He fled to Holland where, in '83,
He died – a sad footnote of history.

The Duke in Scotland

One act of his aroused the King's fury.
After the latter's swift recovery
James was sent off to Scotland, there to 'reign'
As a kind of Viceroy. I'd best explain.
It wasn't a case of exile again,
But trust and promotion, that much is plain.
Shaftesbury showed his disgust and disdain
By summoning the Council, to complain
Of this dubious honour. Charles saw red,
Dismissing the Earl. It has to be said
That the King had been oddly indulgent
In appointing Shaftesbury President
(Of his Council). It was Charles' strategy,
However, to get the Whigs on side, see?
Divide and rule. A subtle policy.

While Charles was winning the battle down south,
James, you'd imagine, was down in the mouth.

Not so. The Duke proved a surprise success.
Up north for two and a half years, no less,
He governed wisely, with skill and *finesse.*
Scotland was riddled with warring factions.
One of his more intelligent actions

Was to seek to balance the interests
Of Scottish chieftains. The stiffest of tests!

In the field of religion, again,
James' rule was a triumph (well, in the main).
He displayed a measured toleration
Of moderate dissent – confirmation
Of his natural bent. This he combined
With less sensitive treatment, unrefined
And callous, where he uncovered cases
Of explosive extremism. Places
Such as Airds Moss, way down in the south-west,
Harboured 'Cameronians', a foul nest
Of militant Covenanters. At best,
James could be called a saviour; at worst,
A foul torturer, his name ever cursed.

James the Second, the Forgotten King

The Duke loved the Scottish Parliament,
A compliant body. This, of course, meant
That (unlike its turbulent counterpart
In England) it lacked teeth, brains, guts and heart!
James was enamoured, and little wonder.
He weighed in at first, all blood and thunder,
But quickly twigged that it would rubber-stamp
His every wish. James, the little scamp,
Exploited this for all he was worth. So,
He secured with ease (good for the ego)
An Act that effectively guaranteed
(In Scotland, at least) his right to succeed.
He managed to procure extra money,
Through taxation, for the Army. Funny,
But Charles would simply never have tried it.
His Parliament? They'd have denied it.

Another parallel of interest:
The Scots passed their own version of the 'Test'.
All MPs, office holders and clergy
Were sworn, as a matter of urgency,
To uphold the rights of their liege the King
(His prerogatives and everything);
To alter not a jot of Church or State
(This all too horrible to contemplate);
And ever to stick to the Protestant creed,
Never to abandon it (strictly no need).

The Duke's stint in Scotland is dogged, of course,
With controversy. Macaulay (the sauce!)
Dubbed him a "brutal sadist". Now, I've read
That the Lord Macaulay (though nobly bred)
Was a Whig. What else, then, would he have said?
More generous students of history
Have judged James rather more leniently.
Your average new-age English Tory
Saluted him as a success story.

Rhyming History

James riding high

Thereby hangs a tale. If only he'd learned…
By the time (March '82) James returned,
The Tories (anti-Exclusionists,
Anglicans and arch-traditionalists)
Were in the ascendant. Charles, at long last,
Was finally persuaded to hold fast
To the 'old ways'. The Earl of Clarendon
(Remember him? Pompous, never much fun,
But as sound as they come) had always known
That the surest way to secure the throne
Was through support of the Anglican Church.

Now the King saw sense and left in the lurch
Dissenters… Catholics… all but the cream –
Viz. the Church of England. James, it would seem,
Was now to be trusted, though Catholic,
As Charles' successor. So, what made him tick?
His commitment (bizarre and fantastic)
To the Anglican Church! The Duke's success
Against Scottish dissent (this is my guess)
Left folk at home to take James at his word.
The Church would be safe in his hands. Absurd.

Be that as it may. For the next four years,
Until Charles' untimely death, James quelled fears
That he was anything but straight and true.
I'd have distrusted the Duke, wouldn't you?
Yet, as Charles grew more lax and indulgent
(Not in religion – that's not what I meant),
James took on the mantle of government.
The Test Acts were forgotten. He was back
On the Privy Council. He had the knack
Of 'wheedling his way'. He'd had the sack
As Lord High Admiral. He was restored.
The Commons, we know, James deeply deplored.

No longer an issue! Parliament
Had been dissolved for the last time. This meant
That Charles (and his younger brother) could rule
Free from constraints. This suited the old fool.
With Shaftesbury and his Whigs on the run,
The King, it appeared, would rather have fun
Than bother himself with affairs of state –
The impression he gave at any rate.

Charles now indulged his love of horse-racing,
Hawking (at least when the air was bracing)
And loose women (which goes without saying).

He left government wholly in James' hands.
The Duke's authority, one understands,
Was absolute. An exaggeration?
Perhaps, but broadly the situation.

The Oxford Parliament

At Oxford the abrupt dissolution
Of Charles' last Parliament (solution
To his worst nightmare) had been a great *coup*.
Another nail in the Whig coffin – phew!
He crowned this political masterstroke
With a demand (Charles was a canny bloke)
That a declaration should be broadcast
From all Church pulpits in the land: now, at last,
The great triumvirate of liberty,
Religion and, of course, property
Was safe from the threat of rebellion.

Whig historians like Trevelyan
Are wont to cavil at this clever move
As exploitative. Not so. I approve.
Charles simply seized the initiative.
Whigs were a menace. Something had to give.

The spectre of Civil War (a disgrace)
Was an awesome threat to wave in the face
Of a fearful and credulous nation.
It was the King's very Restoration
That had finally put paid to schism
And the foul taint of republicanism.

The danger now, though: absolutism.
Who cared? Tories were in the ascendant,
King Charles secure on his throne, resplendent.

The Rye House Plot

Shaftesbury's flight, in 1682,
To Holland left the Whigs in quite a stew.
The Rye House Plot (an aberration:
The alleged planned assassination
Of Charles and James) gave the King an excuse
To purge them further. Some call it abuse.
They could be right. Algernon Sidney died
For his part in the plot. Algie was tried,
Convicted of treason and beheaded.
Judge Jeffreys was the one they all dreaded.
Sidney got him! The trial was nonsense,
Based on the flimsiest of evidence.

William, Lord Russell, was another
Executed for his pains. Oh, brother:
Find a Whig leader, decapitate him,
And Bob's your uncle. As if on a whim,
The Popish Plot (like an action replay)
Was run in reverse, a cruel display
Of anti-Whig mania. To this day
It's less than certain whether poor Sidney
(He never confessed) or Will were guilty.
The Earl of Essex died in the Tower,
By his own hand. A sad, sorry shower

Were the Whigs. Essex, we're told, slit his throat.
An honourable man, a peer of note,
He was described by Evelyn as "wise…
"Sober… and pondering". It's no surprise,
As an ex-leading Exclusionist,
That they bayed for his blood. You get the gist.

Monmouth's shame

The odds on 'King' Monmouth also lengthened.
James' position was further strengthened
By the suspicion (hard truth, rather)
That Monmouth had schemed against his father –
A participant in the Rye House Plot.
Did Charles credit it? Well, he'd rather not,
But the evidence was plain and pressing.
The King's favourite son? Too distressing.

Yet Monmouth saved himself by confessing.
Charles, amazingly, offered his blessing.

Monmouth threw himself at his father's feet,
Wept and was pardoned, forgiveness complete.
Only a wee while later, though, his friends
Denied his complicity. It depends
Which books you read (it's rather hit and miss)
Whether Monmouth himself authorised this.
But Charles was livid when his son withdrew
His confession. Whatever one's view,
James, Duke of Monmouth, was exiled abroad,
In shame and dishonour. His sad reward
Was never to see his father again.

Monmouth's loss was the Duke of York's clear gain.
The darling of the Exclusionists,
His star was in eclipse. Was he much missed?
I should say not. His uncle's arch-rival,
Now at stake was his very survival.
As James was walking increasingly tall,
Folk took no notice of Monmouth at all.
He slunk off to Holland to meditate
On his rotten luck – and to watch and wait.

Tory ascendancy

The new Tory trend continued apace
With control of the boroughs (a disgrace) –
Corrupt and crooked, I have to admit.
You want skulduggery? Well, this was it.
The move was blatant, on the Tories' part,
To oust the Whigs from power. They took heart
From the recent precedent of London –
A city stiff with Whigs, all said and done.
Shaftesbury's acquittal, to Charles' fury,
Resulted (true) from an all-Whig jury.
The City's charter was declared forfeit
(All rather dull, just take my word for it),
And was then redrafted in such a way
(Rigged, I call it) so the Tories held sway.

Smaller town charters were challenged and, hey,
The Whigs in their boroughs too had their day.
The King effectively held a veto
Over political appointments. So,
When the time came round for the election
Of a Parliament, the selection
Of candidates (believe this if you will)
Was a royal stitch-up – a bitter pill
For the Whigs; a fillip for the Tories.
Vote-rigging: one of the age-old stories.

This explains how James' first Parliament
Was thin on Whigs and low on dissent –
Tory to its bones. I'm sorry to say,
This was an edge that he tossed away.
Correction. I said James' 'first' Parliament.
His 'only' that should have read, in the event.

The benefits that he enjoyed stacked up.
Sadly, though, James was an arrogant pup –
Yet another Stuart disappointment!
As Duke of York, even the appointment
Of bishops was within his gift. The King
(Still Charles) set up this commission thing –
Most of whose members were pretty right wing,
Including his brother – to oversee
Promotions to the episcopacy.
This enabled James to choose men whom he,
As King, could trust: staunch Tories to a man,
High Anglican stalwarts. Not a bad plan.

The King is dead! Long live the King!

So, when King Charles the Second breathed his last
(A sudden stroke), were Anglicans downcast?
Tories and Protestants, were they aghast?
Apparently not, strange as this might seem.
They welcomed King James as if in a dream.

A dreadful Papist, whom five years before
They'd set upon as rotten to the core
And sought to bar from his inheritance –
Foe to the Church of England, friend to France –
The country now embraced with a will.
It seemed, in faith, that Time had stood still.

A fine start

In contrast to the late King's negligence,
Intemperance and cool indifference
To hard graft stood the new King's diligence,
Sobriety, economy, sound sense
And straight talking. Slender intelligence,
Backstairs debauchery, intransigence –
To say nothing of downright arrogance –
All were overlooked. It soon turned sour,
But James, for now the hero of the hour,
Denied a taste for arbitrary power.

King James confronted the issues head on.
Though never a man to be put upon,
He published for the 'education'
Of his people, this declaration
To his Council: it would be his "endeavour"
(I do have to say, the wording was clever)
"To preserve this government in Church and State
"As it is by law established". Far too late
Did Englishmen discover (a bitter pill)
This warranty to be far from James' true will.

His words, let us say, were 'conditional'.
Be that as it may, the King (for good or ill)
Would take all due care to "defend and support"
The Church of England. This was to come to nought,
After many a battle fiercely fought,
But for now men rejoiced. They swallowed it all,
Hook, line and sinker. James' precipitous fall

James the Second, the Forgotten King

Is unparalleled in English history,
His character to blame (no great mystery).

I've no doubt at all that he meant what he said.
Within four years, however, the King had fled –
Over the water to France. England's Great Seal
He dropped in the Thames. It hardly seems real.

Part of the new King's initial appeal
Lay in his 'difference'. His elder brother
Was a law unto himself, like no other.
James was transparent, completely straightforward.
Loyal subjects need fear nothing untoward.
From the declaration quoted above,
It's plain James expected deference – nay, love.
This was his due. As King he would persever
To defend the right of the Crown, but never
"Invade any man's property", ever.

Who, after that, could fear this Catholic King?
Church and State James would preserve – everything.

He meant not a word of it. Sickening.
Even as England's pulse was quickening,
James was planning a papist takeover –
No cursory Catholic makeover,
But a sea-change in the nation's affairs.
Protestants had been taken unawares,
Tories and Anglicans, duped to a man.
It wasn't that long before the fun began.

I must confess I never was a fan
Of King James the Second – an also-ran,
Self-centred and blinkered. But, if I can,
I shall do my level best to be fair.
The most learned of scholars, as elsewhere,
Tend on this issue to be divided:
Whether the King (I'm still undecided)

Rhyming History

Advocated freedom for Catholics
To convert the country to Rome (mud sticks)
Or simply to raise public awareness
Of the plight of Papists (simple fairness).

All that's to come. Our friend, John Evelyn,
Welcomed the new era James ushered in,
The King "affecting neither profaneness
"Nor buffoonery". John favoured plainness
And morality over idle sport,
Noting, early, "the face of the whole Court
"Exceedingly changed". The late King, indeed,
Was "obscurely buried" (sinners take heed)
"Without any manner of pomp". Rotten,
In my view, that Charles was "soon forgotten".

"Everything is very happy here,"
Wrote the Earl of Peterborough. "Hear, hear!"
They chimed. Such was the general refrain.
"I doubt not but to see a happy reign."

James cashed in on this favourable start.
Parliament he found in rare good heart.
The King was voted all his revenues –
For life. For James this was very good news.
How, you may ask, could the Commons refuse?
Quite easily, I'd hazard, but take note,
Pray, of James' peevish tone (again I quote):
He'd strongly resent a contrary vote,
For a term of years only. For "this would be
"A very improper method to take with me".

Dogmatic? Dictatorial? Or what?
His manner was his undoing, the clot.
Fix my allowance (this the gist of it)
Or else I'll throw a little hissy fit.
The Commons, for now, swallowed it in one –
Craven and cowardly, all said and done.

What's this I can hear? It's brave John Pym,
Turning in his grave. Remember him?

Monmouth's rebellion

One stroke of luck gave James an early boost.
You've heard of chickens coming home to roost –
Well, James, Duke of Monmouth, the King's nephew,
Was shortly to cause a rare old to-do
By mustering a scratch invasion force
To challenge his uncle. Crazy, of course.
His strategy and timing were all wrong.
The new monarch, as we've seen, was 'on song'
And commanded the heights (if not for long).

Parliament marked the occasion
Of Monmouth's foolhardy invasion
By voting a large increase for the King.
The rebellion was, if anything,
A timely and convenient blessing!
James (the nephew) was in the Netherlands,
Egged on by chums (ill-informed firebrands)

Rhyming History

To reckon his uncle woefully weak,
His kingdom all a-totter, so to speak –
Simply because the King was Catholic
And he, James Monmouth, was not. Fantastic!

Four years on, things would look quite different:
A populace seething with discontent;
A formal invitation to invade;
And men prepared to call a spade a spade.

Monmouth fully expected folk to rise
In defence of his 'right'. Surprise, surprise:
When he landed his paltry force at Lyme
(Eighty 'troops', a handful of boats), his crime
Was palpable. Rebellion – no more,
No less. You could barely call it a war.
Pathetic. An amateur indulgence.
His claim to the throne? Pure, idle nonsense.

The Duke's aims were over-ambitious,
Foolhardy, vain and injudicious.
He hoped (or somehow was led to expect)
The English army, in droves, to defect.

To boost his cause was the added prospect
Of a simultaneous uprising
In Scotland. It wasn't so surprising
That the Earl of Argyle's adventure failed.
His plans for rebellion were derailed
When James' forces received advance warning
Of his landing. Few went into mourning
When the errant Earl was executed.
Scottish politics are convoluted,
But James was stronger north of the border
Than some imagined. The odd marauder,
Certainly... But chaos and disorder
Are not the fittest terms that spring to mind
For James' reign in Scotland, I think you'll find.

James the Second, the Forgotten King

So, instead of the King's troops being split,
They had one focus – and Monmouth was it!
James' army only numbered, nonetheless,
8,000 men, tops. I'm bound to confess,
By European standards this was small.
In the event it mattered not at all.
Thousands of rough yokels flocked to the cause
Of the 'Pretender'. Since the Civil Wars
The West Country had been strong in support
Of non-conformity. Their last resort
Was rebellion, but they weren't the sort,
These sons of the soil, to band together
Into a fighting force. Who knows whether,
Had he stuck to his guns, the wretched Duke
Might just have made it… He earned the rebuke
Of his supporters by losing his nerve.
They'd hailed him King (which he didn't deserve)
And, armed to the teeth with sickles and scythes,
Declared for Monmouth. Distinctly unwise.

The honest labourers of Somerset,
The ploughboys of Devon and West Dorset,
Paid a painfully heavy price, poor sods.
They went like lambs to the slaughter. Ye gods!

Their betters, the gentry (West Country Whigs),
Kept their heads down. If they did care two figs
For Monmouth (likely enough) they were wise
Not to let on. One can merely surmise
Their instincts told them the time wasn't ripe
For open revolt. The Duke was all hype.

Monmouth led his rabble of an army
Towards Bristol. It would have been barmy
To march on London (at this stage, at least) –
Anywhere, frankly, towards the south-east –
But Bristol was feebly fortified
And rich with sympathisers. Had he tried,

Our friend might well have taken the city
With comparative ease. More's the pity
(From a rebel point of view), he funked it,
Withdrawing to Bridgwater. Did he quit?
No. Though Monmouth's confidence, bit by bit,
Ebbed away as the King's forces closed in,
He dreamt nonetheless that still he could win –
Given some luck and a following wind.

The Battle of Sedgemoor

He was anything if not determined,
Resolving to launch an assault, by night,
At Sedgemoor. Now, if I've got my sums right,
The rebels still outnumbered James' forces –
In men, at least (not sure about horses).
Under cover of dark a surprise attack
Could scatter the enemy. No going back.

The King's troops had just settled in for the night
When a rather jumpy rebel took fright
And fired his trusty musket by mistake.
James' men (still half-asleep for pity's sake)
Seized their weapons, though fearfully prepared
For sudden, violent death. Most were spared.

For Monmouth's wretched rag-bag, sad to say,
Had left their maps at home. They lost their way,
Stranded on open ground. At break of day
All were exposed as sitting ducks. Well, hey –
They learnt their lesson: never to rebel
Against the Lord's anointed. Truth to tell,
Those who missed being felled by musket fire,
Or hacked to death with swords, were to aspire
To a fate more awful, deadlier by far,
At the Bloody Assizes. An abattoir
The West Country resembled, as 'justice'
(Ha!) was wrought on the insurgents. Mark this:

Dozens of poor peasants were hanged or shot
Without a hearing. James, like it or not,
Sanctioned this outrage. The King was advised –
By Chief Justice Jeffreys (few were surprised) –
That those who'd proclaimed his nephew as King
Could be hanged without trial. A dreadful thing.

This would act "as a terror to the rest".
King James agreed. I venture to suggest,
If Kings can't be fair they should try their best.
Well, James comprehensively failed the test.

The price of rebellion

The Bloody Assizes (so-called) were worse.
Justice? Jest not! This was quite the reverse.
The Lord Chief Justice gave good cause to curse.
Jeffreys and his cronies, mere acolytes,
Rode roughshod over fairness, human rights

Rhyming History

(As we'd call them today) and due process.
They were out to convict, no more, no less.
The sad victims of these treason trials
Were afforded no say, no denials,
No defence. Jeffrey's victims, by the score –
Two hundred, three hundred, possibly more –
Were executed by hanging, drawing
(I'll explain that shortly) and quartering.
Imagine anything more eye-watering.

The process was as follows… Skip this bit
If you're squeamish, it won't take a minute.

Traitors were hanged, then cut down, still alive
(Those close to death they fought hard to revive),
Only then to be eviscerated
(Their innards torn out: this titillated
The baying spectators apparently).
Their bodies were then dismembered, squarely,
Into four quarters, hence the description.
This was doled out, as if by prescription,
To those poor creatures adjudged guilty
Of treason. The corpses were foul, filthy
And smelly. An affront to good hygiene,
They would fast turn putrid, rancid and green.

So, a further stage in this rank process
Was for the 'bits' (grim, I have to confess)
To be boiled, including the head, no less,
Then tarred (a preservative, I suppose).
I won't say they smelt as sweet as a rose;
It meant, though, that each foul traitor's remains
Could be set on spikes, complete with their brains,
As a lesson to others. The quarters –
In full view of wives, mothers and daughters –
Were posted up for the whole world to see
In every corner of the West Country.

James the Second, the Forgotten King

The business took ages, reportedly –
This savage procedure the epitome
Of rampant, judicial cruelty.
A maximum of ten victims a day
Could be served in this obnoxious way.

Preparations for the awful slaughter
Were precisely drawn: the boiling water
(Salted, for the better preservation
Of the heads); axes (for separation
Of the said quarters); the gallows, of course;
Oxen to draw the carts (or the odd horse);
Tar (in copious quantities); sharp pikes
(On which to display the severed heads); spikes
And knives (with which to gouge the entrails out):
A costly undertaking, have no doubt.

"Enough!" the sensitive among you cry.
"What of the Duke?" you ask, the reason why
So many noble peasants had to die –
Monmouth the brave, the handsome! Sad to say,
The coward took to horse and rode away.
The 'darling of the people', Monmouth fled,
Dumped on his followers, left them for dead.

Monmouth's fate

I'm relieved to say, he too lost his head.
King Charles the Second's eldest bastard son
Was a lightweight varlet, all said and done.
Within three days of the rout at Sedgemoor
He was found in a ditch. Need I say more?
Dishevelled, famished, " 'tis said he trembled" –
Evelyn's expression. He resembled
A scruffy rustic, with a rough grey beard.
It was Uncle Jimmy whom now he feared.

He found the King in no forgiving mood.
He'd called James a usurper (pretty rude),
Even hinting he murdered his brother,
King Charles. What with one thing and another
(Responsibility for the Great Fire
Included: Monmouth was such a fine liar),
It comes as no surprise that the Duke's pleas
Fell on deaf ears. Monmouth dropped to his knees,
Begging, pleading, as he'd done in times past
Before Charles, his pa. These tears were his last.

His cries were in vain. James' mind was made up.
His slimy nephew, this infamous pup,
Paid dear for his treachery. And that's why,
In '85, the 15th of July,
The Duke was despatched to the block – to die!

It took a while. Executioner Ketch,
An incompetent knave and blundering wretch,

Brought down his axe five times on Monmouth's neck,
Yet still couldn't sever it. Flippin' heck!
He needed a knife to finish him off.
"Debauched by lust," wrote Evelyn (don't scoff),
"Seduced by crafty knaves", he was (sad truth)
"A lovely person", a most "darling" youth.

On the scaffold this "Perkin" made no speech.
He had no axe to grind, no wish to preach.
He penned a simple letter to the King
Renouncing his claim to everything:
The throne; even his legitimacy –
His ma had never been married, you see.
The rogue asked James to show kindness to his wife,
Long since abandoned. So ended his wild life.

The King was later to accuse Jeffreys
Of bringing "great obloquy", if you please,
Upon his "royal clemency". And yet,
On his Honour's return from Somerset,
James appointed the brute Lord Chancellor.
It all depends which version you prefer.
I reckon the King backed Jeffreys' campaign.
You know the old saying: no pain, no gain.

The King and Catholicism

King James declined to take the sacrament
At his Coronation. To what extent
This neglect gave rise to hostile comment
Among Anglicans one can only guess.
It appears he simply couldn't care less.
Indeed, the scoundrel celebrated Mass
Just hours before he was crowned. Silly ass:
Clumsy, insensitive, wilful and crass.
He'd already pledged to Parliament,
Hypocrite as he was, his firm intent
To preserve, in essence, "this government

"In Church and State". To this laudable end
He would strain every sinew to defend
The Church of England. Anglicans rejoiced.

What the new King, however, scarcely voiced
Was his parallel determination
To show indulgence and toleration
Towards Catholics. James' reputation
As a staunch Papist had split the nation
During the Exclusion crisis. Now –
Who knows why or wherefore, but anyhow –
Men were prepared to take James at his word
When he pledged to support the Church. Absurd.

At his Coronation the worst occurred,
Raising some eyebrows. The crown slipped off his head.
The illest of omens, it has to be said.

James the Second, the Forgotten King

The King resolved to promote the interests
Of Catholics by dispensing with the 'Tests'.
Papists suffered a manifest injustice,
Barred, as they were, from political office.
James viewed monarchy as a sacred service –
God's work. The sweeping away of prejudice
Was right and just. It's hard to argue with this.
James was the model of a progressive King,
A 'modern' monarch. He lacked only one thing:
An instinct for the 'art of the possible'.

For James considered himself unstoppable.
First, he urged his Parliament to repeal
The penal laws. Who couldn't see the appeal
Of tolerance for Catholics? Then (phase two),
Repeal of the Test Acts. You'd think, wouldn't you,
That James might have foreseen the naked terror
That seized his subjects. A serious error.
However illogical their dread might be,
They feared that the papist constituency,
Delivered from their religious fetters,
Would swiftly supplant their Protestant 'betters',
Propelling an unsuspecting nation back
To Queen 'bloody' Mary's reign. Thumbscrews, the rack,
The stake… Anglicans had an uncanny knack
Of demonising the anti-Christ, the Pope.
Rumour, fancy and lies. James hadn't a hope.

The King and his ministers

The King's choice of ministers was suspect.
He chose advisers, as you might expect,
Who showed preparedness to go along
With his papist policies, right or wrong.
The Earl of Sunderland, a case in point,
A renegade, who didn't disappoint,
Was a time-serving toad. It may seem odd,
But he'd favoured Exclusion. Good God!

Rhyming History

The Earl was astute, not to say wily,
To bounce back from that. Oily and smiley,
The snake buttered up Charles, then James. Slyly,
He wormed his way into the King's good books,
Converting (yes, it's as bad as it looks)
To the Catholic faith. It's surprising
(No, sad), but it worked. 'Apostatising'
They call it. Sunderland only did it
To please his Majesty, the hypocrite.

As James blundered on, Sunderland conspired
To dump on his rivals. Far from admired,
He was nonetheless feared. One enemy
Was Rochester (dyed-in-the-wool Tory) –
The King's brother-in-law and younger son
Of the great Clarendon. There was no one
More steeped in the Anglican tradition
Than he. His political position
Was ever more steadily undermined
As James became increasingly inclined
To trust only Catholics. Able, wise
And astute, it comes as little surprise
That Rochester (Lord Treasurer, no less)
Anticipated the terrible mess
The King was making of public affairs.

James, he saw, was stumbling unawares
Towards doom. Unlike some, he vocalised
His doubts and concerns. Rochester advised
That Papists were far too influential
In Council. The King should be far more mindful
Of the fears of his Protestant subjects,
Wary (nay, jealous) of papist prospects.
Apply the brakes on Catholic projects!
Moreover (which didn't please James overmuch),
He should show more sympathy towards the Dutch.
The King's pro-French stance, like that of his brother,
Caused greater discomfort than any other.

Protestant panic

This was most particularly the case
When Louis of France (a perfect disgrace)
Revoked, at a stroke, the Edict of Nantes.
It's hard to think of anything (I can't)
More calculated to stir up panic
Among Protestants. The mood was manic.

For nigh on one hundred years Huguenots
Had enjoyed protection (fragile, God knows)
Against religious persecution
By the Catholic state. A solution
(Of sorts), the Edict stood the test of time,
Until Lou committed the heinous crime
Of revoking it. Flooding in from France
Came tales of woe which, even at first glance,
Confirmed all Protestants in their worst fears.
Non-Catholics in England were all ears.

'85 was one of those dismal years
Disfigured by religious outrage.
The scale of the scandal is hard to gauge,
But up to 80,000 refugees –
From a mere one million, if you please –
Sought asylum in England. Others left
For Holland (even Switzerland), bereft.

James expected the displaced Huguenots
To worship (this really gets up my nose)
According to Anglican rite. Suppose
(For the sake of argument) you'd just fled
France, forced at rapier-point from your bed,
Or even at risk of losing your head.

Would you choose England? Or somewhere, instead,
Which offered you genuine freedom? Shame
On James, I say. It wasn't in his name
That the refugees were made welcome. No –
He sat on the fence, the crafty so-and-so.

The King's advantage squandered

Be that as it may. Within one short year
The King had contrived to offend (oh, dear)
His most compliant supporters. Who cared?
Not he! His brother would never have dared,
Nor his dad (yes, I do mean Charles the First),
But somehow James managed to do his worst.
He spurned the best advice of his allies,
Men like Rochester, who (surprise, surprise)
Got their marching orders; Halifax, too;
Middleton; Queensberry – more than a few.
It smacked of a covert Catholic *coup.*
What in God's name could the Anglicans do?

Sit it out was one answer. James was old,
In seventeenth century terms, we're told:

One's early fifties then were quite an age.
Wait for his death, for Fate to turn the page
And usher in a new, glorious reign
Under Protestant Mary, the King's plain,
Moral and upright daughter. Then again,
What if James' own Queen (the other Mary)
Should breed? Anglicans were rightly wary,
Despite the fact that since her marriage
The Queen had suffered from miscarriage
(Twice) and, of her four children born alive,
Just one had enjoyed the strength to survive –
Before dying in infancy, sadly.

Trouble with the Anglicans

James, moreover, was behaving badly
Towards the Anglicans. In '86   **1686**
He decreed (up to his usual tricks)
That preachers should desist from knocking Rome
And stick to 'safer' subjects. This hit home
When James (an act of utter recklessness)
Ordered the Bishop of London, no less,
To suspend a local rector, John Sharp,
For preaching against Rome. Sorry to carp,
But this was a grand folly, high-handed
And truculent. The King was left stranded
When Compton (the Bishop) stoutly refused.

James saw red, professing himself ill used.
How dare these Anglicans disobey him?
So he raised a warrant (this on a whim)
To set up an Ecclesiastical
Commission. It may sound fantastical,
But this new body assumed James' powers
To discipline clerics. Within hours
(Well, a few weeks) Compton had been hauled in
And dismissed from his bishopric. A sin,
I call it, but the poor soul couldn't win.

This proved to be a most frightful error
On the King's part. Compton was a terror,
And played a leading and enlightened part
In James the Second's downfall. So, take heart.

Every member was the King's crony.
Headed by Jeffreys (Catholic phoney),
The Commission boasted Sunderland,
Another 'convert'. Cheap and underhand.
How could the King have failed to be aware
How this would play with Protestants? Despair,
Horror, dismay… Far more than they could bear.

From a modern standpoint it's quite unfair
That Catholics suffered exclusion
From public office. The profusion
Of discriminatory rules and laws
Disgusts us today. James merits applause –
For effort. His motives were far from base.
His methods, though, were a total disgrace.
His politics: hopeless! He forced the pace
And by '88 he had lost his place –
His Crown, his kingdom, his birthright, the lot.
In colloquial terms, he lost the plot.

Many will say he deserved all he got.
Another mistake that he made (the clot)
Was admitting four staunch Catholic peers
To his Privy Council. This stoked new fears
Among Anglicans and strengthened the hand
Of that wolf in sheep's clothing, Sunderland.

William of Orange watches and waits

James sent his Quaker friend, William Penn –
A man of high honour and acumen –
To Holland to ask his son-in-law there,
William (whose wife, Mary, was James' heir),

To signal approval for the repeal,
In England, of the Test Acts. "Get real!"
Was William of Orange's reply.
He refused point blank. I shall tell you why.

It were sheer madness to identify
Himself (or Mary, who would rather die)
With any measure that flew in the eye
Of English Protestants. His true instinct
Was for toleration. What do you think?
He kept that under wraps. He didn't blink.
Will and his chief adviser, one Bentinck,
Were watching keenly which way the wind blew.

He wasn't exactly plotting a *coup,*
Not yet. But William was well aware
Of the true depth of Anglican despair
Across the Channel. The Prince would be there,

In person, if needed – and invited.
Orange was not a little excited,
But gave away nothing. His firm reply
To his Uncle Jim, it's hard to deny,
Caused grave and serious disappointment.
That graphic phrase 'a fly in the ointment'
Came to apply to William. For now,
He kept a cool head. He'd never kowtow.
The Prince of Orange was deadly, and how!

Oblivious, James just blundered along.
His reforms, he was clear, were all 'on song'.
His realm, to its roots, was Catholic. Wrong!
This belief is significant. The King
Was sure in his heart of one simple thing:
Once rid of the Test Acts and penal laws,
His ears would be deafened by wild applause.
'Protestant' subjects had long been waiting
For liberation! Catholic-baiting,
Bigotry, rancour and venom... at last,
Committed to the flames. Change would come fast,
England restored to the bosom of Rome –
Her one true Church; her spiritual home.

A Declaration of Indulgence

February, 1687,   **1687**
The King published in Scotland, great Heaven,
His first Declaration of Indulgence.
He brooked no opposition, no nonsense.
Based on his "sovereign prerogative",
Scottish Presbyterians, as I live,
Were allowed to meet in private. Quakers –
Dissidents, self-styled 'movers and shakers' –
Were permitted to "meet and exercise"
In their places of worship. Was this wise?
Protestants were wary (surprise, surprise),

James the Second, the Forgotten King

Guarded – nay, hostile; particularly
When the King took the opportunity
(Again, in Scotland) to suspend all laws
Against his Catholic subjects. Applause
Was sporadic, suspicion the cause.

Two months later, pressing on regardless,
James tried the same in England. I confess
To no small measure of admiration
At the King's grit and determination.

A true champion of toleration,
He set his heart on the liberation
Of all men from religious constraints.
Not, of course, that all Catholics were saints,
Quakers neither, other dissidents less.
But James displayed a rare preparedness
To countenance freedom of conscience
To every faith. To him it made sense.

Toleration or hypocrisy?

Somewhat disingenuous, I have to say.
For had the King been allowed to have his way
With respect to liberty of conscience
For Catholics, he'd still have taken offence
At any proposal that he extend
This to other dissenters. Why pretend
Otherwise? Early on, James was no friend
To minority sects. Galling, but true.
It's just that as Anglican anger grew
He turned to these 'remnants'. Well, wouldn't you?

Be that as it may, James' strategy failed.
Dissidents saw red. His plans were derailed.
Old Halifax put his finger on it.
He didn't trust the King one little bit

And fomented the most unholy row.
Dissenters, he warned, "were to be hugged now
"Only that you may be the better squeezed
"At another time". They were being teased,
Cajoled, bribed into supporting the King.
Freedom and toleration were one thing –
Catholicism quite another. Why
Should James, in his infinite wisdom, try
To butter up the dissenters, if not
To isolate the Anglicans? A plot –
It was obvious. So, to stop the rot,
Protestants and dissidents united.

The birth of an heir?

James was quite naturally excited –
Though most, we're told, were far from delighted –
When brought the news that the Queen was with child.
His courtiers were jubilant. They went wild.
The Catholic succession was secure –
One in the eye for William, for sure.
In England this could not have mattered more.
Should Mary bear a son, a healthy boy…

But was her pregnancy a sham, a ploy?
Amazingly some considered it so,
Princess Anne included. Those in the know
Were suspicious of the Queen's 'great belly' –
In Anne's case, perhaps, out of jealousy.

In Holland, of course, these tidings were met
With alarm. Mary was nervous, you bet –
Sceptical too. Letters from her sister
Hinted at something deeply sinister.
Mary (the Queen) was decidedly coy
In Anne's presence. She'd give birth to a boy –
The Court seemed quite sure about that, and yet…
The Queen (so Anne reported) was dead set

On protecting her royal privacy.
Not even Anne was permitted to see
'Naked' evidence of the pregnancy.

Protestants eyed this suspiciously.
Was mischief afoot? Was a boy changeling
Being lined up as a putative King –
Catholic to boot? A terrible thing.
Hardly surprisingly, Princess Mary
And her Dutch husband were rightly wary.
The whole affair was distinctly scary.
Another baby daughter would be fine –
But a boy child? Strewth! He'd be first in line!

How James was so sure we shall never know,
But a son it was to be. As Kings go,
James had a knack of always being right.
He ploughed on, till the last stroke of midnight,
In his long struggle to set England free
From error, prejudice and bigotry.

Rhyming History

Trouble at Oxford

He upset Oxford University
By insisting, rather too forcefully,
On a choice of Catholic President
For Magdalen College. James was hell-bent,
The booby, on causing offence to those
Of whom he was most in need – why, God knows.

The crisis came when the King's nominee
Was rejected by the fellows. Crikey!
This abuse of royal authority –
He'd no such power to appoint, you see –
Was more than matched (in spades, it seems to me)
By the insolence, arrogance and pride
Of the Magdalen fellows. You decide:
Who had right on their side? Fellows or King?
Academic! James gave Jeffreys a ring
(Anachronism, whoops…): "These fellows flout
"The King at their peril! Kick 'em all out!"

This the Commission did. Sunderland,
For reasons not that hard to understand
(Toadying to James), supported the move.
Jeffreys, this time, was less quick to approve.
He feared ejection as a step too far.

What left an even more unsightly scar
Was the draconian declaration –
Far exceeding any expectation –
That the delinquent fellows be deprived
Of clerical livings. How they survived,
I know not. The Commission connived
With the King to punish his enemies
Beyond their deserts. To bring to their knees
Those who annoy you is poor policy.
James' folly was naked for all to see.

Bishops in revolt

The curtain fell in 1688.   **1688**
James, author of his own pitiful fate,
Now upped the stakes. His Declaration
(Of Indulgence) – an aberration
To Anglicans – he ordered to be read
From every English pulpit, force-fed
To many a flock. This rapidly led
To revolt. Six bishops – of Chichester,
St. Asaph, Bath and Wells, Peterborough,
Ely and Bristol – petitioned the King
In person, actually travelling
By riverboat from Lambeth to Whitehall.

They didn't care for his orders at all.
The seventh of their number was Sancroft,
Archbishop of Canterbury. They doffed
Their mitres to his Maj with due respect –
Such perfect manners as you would expect.

Rhyming History

But that was all. They refused, to a man,
To countenance James' demands. So began
The final act in this erratic reign.

Men of the Church were under massive strain.
The bishops published their petition.
The King was livid, his position
Threatened by seven clerics, God be praised!
"A standard of rebellion" they'd raised.
James was "so far incensed at this address"
That he lost his reason – well, more or less.

The nation held its breath. Jeffreys advised –
And Sunderland too (yes, I was surprised) –
That James should back down. Few, though, realised
The scale of his fury. A warning? No.
The renegade bishops would have to go.
The charge was grave: seditious libel.
With each clutching his own little Bible,
Sancroft *et al.* were despatched to the Tower.

Needless to say, heroes of the hour
They fast became. The crowning irony –
Which all bar James could evidently see –
Was that the bishops' breathtaking bravery
In facing up to the King's knavery
(As they clearly saw it) served to unite
The whole Protestant nation in its fight
Against the common foe, the Catholics.

I've no access to Stuart statistics,
But the overwhelming majority
Of English dissidents, apparently –
Except for Catholics, naturally –
Shared the Anglicans' deep hostility
Towards the Indulgence. 'Divide and rule'
James had sought to achieve. Who did he fool?

James the Second, the Forgotten King

If the King in his wisdom could suspend
The Test Acts at will, then where would it end?
He might at pleasure set aside all laws
Ecclesiastical and civil. Pause,
If you will. Draw a deep breath. The applause
To which the bishops' acquittal gave rise
Was well-nigh universal. No surprise,
Then, that dissenters throughout the nation
Shared in the unalloyed jubilation
When the jury decided in favour
Of the clerics. A moment to savour.

Our heroes were mobbed as they left the court.
Evelyn offers a first-hand report:
All the way "from the King's Bench", if you please,
"Was a lane of people… upon their knees",
Right down "to the waterside". Cheers rang out
"As the bishops passed and repassed" – no doubt
Relishing this rare popularity –
"To beg their blessing…" "Bonfires made that night
"And bells ringing" gave James a mighty fright.

It was all "taken very ill at Court".
"Sixty earls and lords" withheld their support
By making "an appearance… on the bench
"In honour of the bishops". Quite a stench
This caused, you may be sure of that. The King
Was on the slide, to my way of thinking.
His courtiers, though inwardly fearful,
Showed themselves "full of courage and cheerful".

The acquittal of the bishops apart,
James for once was in genuine good heart.
To his vast relief and unbridled joy,
The Queen gave birth to a healthy wee boy –
Just two days after the bishops' despatch
To the Tower. This was game, set and match

To the King. The succession, for sure,
In a Catholic line was now secure,
Though the baby 'Prince', so the rumour ran,
Had been smuggled through in a warming pan!

You've heard, of course, of pride before a fall.
Well, James (believe this) even had the gall
To ask the Pope, ever the diplomat,
To stand as sponsor to the little brat.

Anglicans were less than happy with that.
The nation frankly had had enough.
Englishmen were made of sterner stuff.

William at the ready

William of Orange, James' son-in-law,
Had for some years been preparing for war –
Well, 'invasion'. The Prince was wary
Of saying 'war'. Opinions vary,

But had Will, it's generally reckoned,
Declared open war on James the Second
(His uncle too), then disaster beckoned.
How long he'd coveted the English throne,
If indeed he had, is largely unknown.
But the Prince did express himself willing,
If invited, to accept 'top billing' –
To set the poor repressed of England free
From despotism and from popery.

As if butter wouldn't melt! Nobody
Held this to be his uppermost reason.
Will's motives (little less than high treason)
Were deep-rooted, complex and historic.
His early rise had been meteoric.
Leader of his country at twenty-one,
His entire career, all said and done,
Was devoted to the struggle with France.

For this he was ill-equipped, at first glance.
Less like a warrior he couldn't be –
Short of stature, unheroic, ugly...
No, that's not quite fair: 'unprepossessing'
Would be more apt. His lonely, distressing
Childhood (orphaned when he was only ten)
Left him shy and reserved. This best of men
Displayed true merit from a tender age.
Taciturn and rarely given to rage,
He observed the motto, every day,
Of the House of Orange: *je maintiendrai.*
Cool under fire, Prince William's way,
His lifetime pursuit, I'm honoured to say,
Was defence of his homeland, come what may.

Louis the Fourteenth was his deadly foe,
The principal reason (this you should know)
For William's daring invasion.
The French on more than one occasion

Rhyming History

Had brought the Dutch Republic to its knees –
Well, very nearly. Louis, if you please,
Fostered ambitions to hold in thrall
The whole of Europe – enough to appal
The Dutch. They didn't care for this at all.

William was their champion. His skill
In containing Louis, for good or ill,
Endeared him to his people. It was tough,
Nonetheless. Holland's merchants (fair enough)
Were nervous of the Prince and resisted
His warlike policies. They insisted
On trading with the French – until, that is,
Louis himself threw them into a tizz
By banning the import (how mad was this?)
Of herrings from the Netherlands. The Dutch,
Men of the sea, had dug deep and cared much
For their fishing industry. By sheer stealth
Louis had stymied their main source of wealth.
The Dutch merchant classes were now on side
Against France. Commercial suicide
On Louis' part, I'd say – hard to decide
Why or wherefore. Getting cocky, perhaps?
The French were always the oddest of chaps.

A short history of Orange

Orange was a small principality
In far south-eastern France. The Prince, you see,
Had no royal status among the Dutch,
No right to govern the people as such.
It's simply that the Orange family
Had been the ones who, historically,
Had united the various Dutch states
In times of crisis. They weren't potentates
By virtue of descent, but had a knack,
When the Dutch Republic was on the rack,

James the Second, the Forgotten King

Of cutting the mustard. Will's father died
Days before his birth. His ma never tried
To 'fit in'. The sister of Charles the First,
Mary, no fan of the Dutch, roundly cursed
The day she left England. Her son, therefore,
Enjoyed no special rank. Yet he bore
His historic responsibilities
With firm resolve, at home and overseas.

Following his father's death, if you please,
The 'States-General' opted to dispense
With the House of Orange. This made no sense.

Let's go back several generations
And try to forget all those frustrations
Appertaining to the strange history
Of the Netherlands. It's no mystery
How the United Provinces, so-called,
Came about. The Dutch had long been appalled

Rhyming History

By their own sad subservience to Spain.
Those from the north had sought time and again
To throw off the repressive Spanish yoke.
These plucky, independent northern folk
Banded together (no word of a joke)
From provinces such as Holland, Zeeland,
Utrecht (and assorted parts of Friesland),
Along with such cities as Antwerp, Bruges,
Ypres and Breda (the project was huge)
And swore to the Union of Utrecht.

This was historic, as you might expect.
The Union effectively became
The new foundation, in all but name,
Of an independent state. However,
Each city and province (this was clever)
Retained its separate identity
In domestic affairs. Sovereignty
Was preserved to this critical degree –
An accord of some ingenuity.

The Union's objective was defence.
In foreign affairs (this made perfect sense)
Each 'unit' was pledged to act together
In peace and war, whatever the weather.
The pressing need (you spotted this, of course)
Was for one leading, unifying force.
This is where the House of Orange came in.
Many a 'stadtholder' (or Dutch 'king pin')
Were Princes of Orange: William's dad,
Grandfather, great-granddad... The Dutch were glad
Of these brave Princes, Commanders-in-Chief,
Who stood up to Spain. It's beyond belief,
Given his splendid Orange pedigree,
That the Dutch seized the opportunity,
After William the Second's demise,
To sideline his baby son. No surprise,
Perhaps, given his age, but hardly wise.

I reckon it was reprehensible,
Stubborn, blinkered and far from sensible.
The threat from Spain had long been in decline,
With Louis the Fourteenth of France in line
As the new aggressor. All very fine,
But who was expected to stand up tall
Against this menace? No contest at all:
The good old House of Orange once again!
They called on William to take the strain.
He stepped up to the mark at twenty-one:
Dark days for the Dutch; it wasn't much fun.

I hope that's useful by way of background.
The time-line gets muddled sometimes, I've found.
For the sake of clarity please take note:
The Utrecht Union (which gets my vote)
Was well over a century before –
1579. Many a war
Was fought by the brave Dutch, bloody and raw,
In defence of the northern Netherlands.

Now, while his nephew was rubbing his hands,
With some eagerness, across the Channel,
James was nodding. Sunderland (all flannel)
Was still cheerfully advising the King
That intelligence from Holland (shocking
And compelling: massed forces gathering
At all Dutch ports) amounted to nothing –
This as late as September '88.

A son... and an invitation

When I say 'late', I really do mean late.
On June the 30th, the very date
Of the bishops' great acquittal, six peers
And one ex-bishop (inspired, it appears,
By James' conduct and the birth of an heir)
Had written to William, then and there,

Inviting him to bring over a force
To England against the King. Now, of course,
The letter was couched with enormous care,
The signatories all too well aware
Of the danger of their position.
They neither sought James' deposition
(Not openly) nor his exclusion –
Even if this was the conclusion
Likely to be drawn. Who were the seven?

The ex-Bishop of London, great Heaven –
Henry Compton. You may remember him,
The man dismissed by the King, on a whim,
For flatly declining to discipline
John Sharp for preaching (most horrible sin)
An anti-popish sermon. Our Henry,
A thorn in James' side, was proving to be
A highly tenacious enemy.

Henry Sidney (later Earl of Romney)
Was the first and foremost signatory,
The rebels' ringleader. Good for Sidney.

James the Second, the Forgotten King

A dyed-in-the-wool Whig, his family
Were hardly renowned for their loyalty.
Philip (one brother), something of a swell,
Fell under Cromwell's republican spell.
Algie (another) got into a spot
For his alleged part in the Rye House Plot.
Flavour of the month the Stuarts were not.
The prospect of William's invasion
Presented yet another occasion
For this restive family to take arms
Against their King. A man of many charms –
Sidney was strikingly handsome, it's said –
Henry was nonetheless easily led.

The Earl of Devonshire, another Whig,
Added his bold signature. Not a fig
Did he care for his safety. Thinking big,
Too, was the stout-hearted Edmund Russell.
Engaged in many a naval tussle
Under King William (as he became),
The future Earl of Orford made his name
At the critical battle of La Hogue.
Russell signed on the dotted line, the rogue.

Another was the Earl of Shrewsbury,
Charles Talbot, a man of rare quality,
Courage, culture and sensibility.
At a tender age (barely turned twenty),
Talbot threw over Catholicism
And firmly embraced Anglicanism.
Religious infighting and schism
He deplored. As a true-born Catholic
You may well wonder what made Charlie tick.
Who knows? You'd think that his experience
'On the outside' might have made him see sense.
Yet opposed to James he was. On the day
That the Prince of Orange sailed to Torbay,

Rhyming History

The wily Earl was on board by his side –
And he hadn't signed up just for the ride.
Whigs were not the only signatories.
Two at least of the seven were Tories.

Lord Lumley was one, another convert
From Catholicism. He lost his shirt
After openly opposing the King
And his politics. It's quite surprising,
Then, to learn that it was his regiment
That ran Monmouth to ground. His discontent
With the King caused Lumley to be deprived
Of his military command. He thrived
Under William, under Queen Anne too –
Nay, even under George the First. He knew,
Did Richard Lumley, which way the wind blew.

The Earl of Danby

The seventh to sign was Thomas Danby.
Remember him? Thomas came in handy
During Charles the Second's perilous reign,
When debt was causing a terrible strain.
A whizz with figures, he saved Charles' bacon –
His rock, his economic salvation.

He fell foul of the Whigs, and was hated
By James too, who never contemplated
Restoring him to favour. You'll recall,
However, that Danby (before his fall)
Had arranged the marriage of Mary
To William. Nothing airy-fairy
About Danby! Robust and hard-headed,
The match that all good Catholics dreaded
Danby designed. A canny kind of bloke,
This was his political masterstroke.
Leave Louis the Fourteenth to huff and puff
All he pleased, the union was enough

James the Second, the Forgotten King

To confound the Catholics and breathe life
Into Anglican dreams. Will and his wife
Were the new Protestant alternative –
And so it proved. The good Earl, as I live,
Exploited his advantage to the hilt.

Sixty years old, he wasn't one to wilt.
He brought most of the north of England out
For the Prince (not short of a bit of clout),
With nobody left in the slightest doubt
Where Danby's loyalties lay. His reward
Was well measured: the Prince could ill afford
To ignore a figure of Danby's flair.
Tom's influence was felt everywhere
In government in the early nineties,
As he shouldered responsibilities
Well in excess of those that he'd discharged
Under Charles. His reputation enlarged,
Danby for his pains became Duke of Leeds –
His wealth and gains far exceeding his needs.

Support for William in England

Seven influential men, and yet
None the highest in the land. You can bet
That William was nervous. He is said,
Indeed, to have spoken of his deep dread
And terrible disquiet. Nonetheless,
Here was a letter. He had to confess
That this frank and open demonstration
Of support, this overt invitation
From a broad cross-section of the nation,
Gave succour to his hopes. For some months past,
Others, with their numbers increasing fast,
Had 'intimated' (no stronger than that)
They'd be more than happy to 'have a chat'
With the Prince should ever the need arise.
Halifax was one such (this no surprise),

Rhyming History

John Churchill (James' favourite) another,
Clarendon (Rochester's elder brother),
And even Rochester himself, we're told.
Stout chaps – never knowingly undersold!

There was now every indication
That the greater body of the nation
Would rally to Will's support. There were fears
Among the people, of course. Three short years
Since, Monmouth's rising had ended in tears –
Rebel corpses hung from every tree
The whole length and breadth of the West Country.

Moreover the strength of the King's army
(In numbers, at least) had increased fourfold.
In spirit? Well, rather less so, we're told.
Indeed, there'd been rumours of robust cheers
From army encampments, raucous "hear, hears",
At the bishops' acquittal. It appears
That William held a very strong hand,
And well he knew it. But pray understand:
Even if invasion went as planned –
A favouring wind, a good place to land –
The Prince could easily still be unmanned
By Louis the Fourteenth in his absence.
Remember, if you will, the threat from France.
Once William's back was turned, the French King
Could advance his army, all guns blazing,
Into the *Pays-Bas* – his for the taking.

William's fears

Lucky for Will (and this was amazing)
Events in Europe caused a diversion.
There was a deep and growing aversion
To Louis right across the continent,
Bred of a blend of envy, discontent

James the Second, the Forgotten King

And fear. Habsburg Emperor Leopold
Was terribly vexed (at least, so we're told)
By the French King's bellicose intentions
In Teutonic territories. Tensions
Were running pretty high along the Rhine.
Sundry German princes agreed to sign
Accords with our William in defence
Of their respective borders (this made sense)
Should Louis of France give cause for offence.

It wasn't only Protestant nations
That gave vent to their latent frustrations.
Spain was supportive of William's cause.
Even the Pope led a round of applause
At the prospect of Louis' bloody nose –
Though why he was bothered, nobody knows.

As for Louis himself, he offered aid
To James, who refused it. James was afraid
(With good reason) of the adverse effect
On opinion at home. Thus he wrecked
His chances. The King was in a cleft stick.
To ask cousin Louis, a Catholic,
To bring to England a foreign army
In defence of the realm… Sorry: barmy!
This, if nothing else, would have fomented
Open rebellion. Well prevented.

Yet Louis knew (he was nobody's fool)
It was just a tad risky, as a rule,
To sally forth to fight a foreign war
Without securing your borders. Therefore,
One strategy to which the French held fast –
At least, that is, until the very last –
Was armed takeover of the Netherlands.
William's giddy and foolhardy plans

Held out a golden opportunity.
Trouble, though, was brewing in Hungary
And surrounding areas. King Louis,
Aggressive, expansionist and greedy,
Altered course. Never one to hesitate,
He mobilised, before it was too late,
His armies into the Palatinate –
All four of them. The details you don't need,
But off went the French with indecent speed.

Preparations for invasion

William, as sure as eggs, took good heed.
His plans at last were reaching fruition.
Focused, resolved, a man on a mission,
The Prince was ready. His invasion fleet
Comprised some sixty warships (no mean feat),
With 15,000 soldiers – infantry
(Eighteen battalions), and cavalry
(Over 4,000). Think of the horses!
All the supplies required for these forces!
Food, uniforms, guns, brandy, tobacco –
Even salted herrings, I'll have you know;
Medicines, hay for the horses, new boots –
Though few, I've been assured, were raw recruits;
Printing presses, too. For the Prince, you see,
Declared himself, with blushing modesty,
The champion of English liberty.

Propaganda was the name of the game.
He repeated the preposterous claim
That the King's new-born son was not his own.
In this belief the Prince was not alone.
He milked the rumour for all it was worth:
The Prince of Wales was of 'dubious' birth,
His pa a dastardly Jesuit priest
Or (lower by far) a miller, at least.

Where one particular story began –
I've already mentioned the warming pan –
I know not. I'm a particular fan
Of William and I'm loth to credit
The Prince with such nonsense. This I admit.

The King's complacency

James at last took notice of the threat. Still,
The Dutchman's chances of success were nil
In the King's considered view. He was glad
Of the approach of autumn. It were mad
At this late season of the year, of course,
To take to sea with an invasion force.
No sane leader of men would run the risk.
Winds by mid-October were at best brisk,

Rhyming History

Tides hazardous, the weather inclement.
The Prince, normally quite intelligent,
Was acting like a fool. Was he crazy?

The King's reasoning was flawed and lazy.
Greatness seldom springs from hesitation.
James had lost the respect of the nation.
When he finally came to realise
The danger, it came as no great surprise
That few men remained to whom he could turn.
Flight was Sunderland's primary concern.
He was fired. Then, of all things to do,
James courted his old adversaries. Who?
The bishops! They'd been mightily ill used.
So, rather predictably, they refused
To "declare an abhorrence" (as the King sought)
"Of the invasion". They were not to be bought.

The Ecclesiastical Commission
Was suspended. James signalled permission
For the restoration of the fellows
Of Magdalen. They say that Time mellows.
Not in this instance. James acted from fear
And few believed he was wholly sincere.
When he did agree to fresh elections,
Few honestly harboured expectations
That he would deliver, particularly
When he argued, somewhat disingenuously,
That the state of national emergency
Rendered elections for Parliament
Impractical – at least for the moment.

James then assured Catholics, in private,
That his word didn't count one little bit!
He promised to do nothing, come what may,
To offend their faith or to spoil their day.
Dishonest and foolish, such was his way.

James the Second, the Forgotten King

Whitehall, reports suggest, was in a spin.
According to our friend, John Evelyn,
"So panic a fear" he could scarce believe.
Then James was blessed with a welcome reprieve.
His nephew had set sail bent on conquest,
But sudden squalls gathering from the west
Had driven the Dutch fleet back into port.
Never downhearted (he wasn't the sort),
William rallied his troops. But the King,
Blind as ever, was soon celebrating.
"I see," he said (somewhat complacently:
James still put his faith, self-evidently,
In Divine Providence), "God Almighty
"Continues in his protection of me."

The Commander of the Fleet, even he
(George Legge, 1st Baron Dartmouth) gleefully
Wrote to James: "Your statesmen may take a nap."
George, I've read, was a convivial chap,
But in naval terms one ghastly mishap.
Mark his conduct. By November the 1st
William's ships were well over the worst –
Re-equipped, minor repairs accomplished,
As fit a fleet as the Dutch could have wished.

Invasion

It's likely the Prince intended to land
In Yorkshire. These things rarely go as planned.
All depends on the wind, you understand.
If it suddenly switches to the east –
And wind can be a pretty fickle beast –
Attend to its dictates and change tack fast.
An easterly breeze? Will wasn't aghast.
He seized the opportunity, at last,
To sail with ease through the Straits of Dover,
Then west down the Channel – a walkover.

Rhyming History

Well, hardly the latter. Luck played its part.
Dartmouth, poor lamb, started off in good heart,
But tended to dither. The English fleet
Was undone. Even had Legge found his feet,
His ships were stuck up the Thames estuary
By the same winds blowing Will westerly
Down the Channel. But what irked James the most
Was the fact that all along the south coast
Folk could clearly read banners promising
To maintain their religion – nothing,
Take note, about Will coming to be King.
Upholding liberty, that was the thing.
It all had a highly plausible ring.

The Dutch armada was a splendid sight.
You could stand on shore (the weather was bright)
And watch the famous flotilla sail past
For seven whole hours, from first to last.
The English fleet was left far, far behind.

James the Second, the Forgotten King

Weather conditions were less than kind
To Dartmouth. Once he'd got out of his bind
And headed west in pursuit of the Dutch,
The wind changed again. William's sure touch
(His luck, rather) held. A westerly breeze
Enabled his entire fleet, with ease,
To tack back into harbour near Torbay –
November the 5th the auspicious day.
The self-same wind, I'm unhappy to say,
Just as Dartmouth's ships were well under way,
Drove them back up the beach. Alackaday!

One truth it's impossible to gainsay
Is that Will was a fortunate blighter.
A fine strategist, a fearless fighter
And an awesome opponent, nonetheless
The Prince himself was the first to confess
To no trifling measure of surprise
At his ease of passage. The enterprise
Was rash, to say the least. Even his spies
Advised caution. He suffered butterflies –
This is true. He was unquiet and fretful,
Confessing that his forebodings were dreadful.

One factor that is often forgotten
Is that James' army (albeit rotten:
Weak-willed and disloyal) was twice the size
Of William's. This comes as a surprise.
Will took some risk. One can only surmise
That the Prince was confident in the trust
He placed in his spies. Believe them he must.
Support for James in the ranks was flaky;
Officers, too: decidedly shaky.
The issue was never put to the test.
James, as we shall see, did his level best
To shun the battle. He declined to fight.
The King lost his nerve and opted for flight.

Rhyming History

Arrival of the Prince of Orange

All this anon. William disembarked
At Brixham and was not a little narked,
After progress to Exeter, to find
No heavyweight supporters of the kind
He'd been led to expect. Don't get me wrong.
His advance so far had been well 'on song'.
He'd met with minimal opposition,
Nothing to suggest that his position
Was anything but strong. The common folk
Had even been ready to josh and joke.

It's reported that Will, upon landing,
Had challenged their native understanding
By saying he had come "for all your goots" –
Fine effort, that, for one with foreign roots –
Whereupon he was met with the riposte:
"Aye, and chattels, too!" Will learnt to his cost,
As the years wore on, that English humour
Was not to his taste. The sorry rumour
Is that the Prince was too dry, serious
And lacking in wit – deleterious,
Sad to say, to his popularity.

Be that as it may. Folk, it seems to me,
Are oh, so fickle – all too keen to praise,
With hindsight, "good King Charles' glorious days!" –
While fast forgetting his immoral ways.
I'm not concerned what anybody says,
But William, however short of wit,
Was worth ten 'Merry Monarchs'. There, that's it!

I'm sure to say the exact opposite
Over Ireland, where he stumbled a bit
(To put it mildly). Billy's legacy
Caused dreadful grief, distress and injury.

The West Country rallies

After kicking his Dutch heels for a while,
The Prince, in time, had better cause to smile.
Sir Edward Seymour, West Country grandee,
Protestant and dyed-in-the-wool Tory,
Came out for Orange, clear for all to see.
His local rival and adversary,
The Marquess of Bath, followed rapidly –
United in defence of liberty
And England's true Church. Down with popery!

Seymour was no revolutionary.
He wasn't opposing the King as such.
He backed the Prince (though wary of the Dutch)
For his pledge to safeguard and guarantee
The Protestant religion. To me
This has the faint whiff of hypocrisy.
How could he have reckoned, seriously,
That James could possibly survive, as King,
Given such 'friends'? Seymour, if anything,
Was hastening James' premature demise.
Had he not declared for Will, my surmise
Is that the Prince's less than noble cause
Might have foundered. After an awkward pause
Will would most likely have upped and turned tail.
Lacking local support? Certain to fail.

The situation, it appears to me,
Was shot through with half-hearted loyalty
And a startling ambiguity.
For mark this: Seymour, William's ally,
Was opposed to granting him the crown. Why?
Well, your guess is as good as mine. Who knows?
His basic Tory instincts, I suppose.
Yet the oath to William and Mary
He swore. Fickle, perverse and contrary.

Rhyming History

Queen Mary?

This instance may be fit to illustrate
The quandary, the agonised debate
And the deep unease that followed James' fall.
Sweet England had no sovereign at all.
Or did she? Mary refused to play ball
When asked to reign alone – in her own right
Or as Regent for her father, whose plight
Was pitiful. Will took it as a slight
That anyone in England should expect
A Dutch Prince to play the role, in effect,
Of his wife's "gentleman usher" – his phrase,
Not mine. For the remainder of his days
The Prince ruled as King William the Third –
Any alternative were too absurd –
First, co-equal with Mary by his side,
Then, after his angelic soul mate died,
Alone, by virtue of the settlement
Thrashed out and ratified by Parliament.

I'm racing ahead. The apparent ease
Of William's progress – even Tories,
As we've witnessed, welcomed him – can blind us
To the worries he faced. There was huge fuss
When it fell to be determined to whom
The crown should be offered. Never assume:
Expectation is rarely midwife
To the event, you can bet your life.

The King dithers

Back to the plot. What was the King doing
The while? Not a lot. Trouble was brewing –
Even he could see that, no arguing.
James was sorely tempted to run away.
Wiser counsels encouraged him to stay.
Who was this Prince of Orange anyway?

James the Second, the Forgotten King

Let the villain come to London and fight!
The poor King suffered a serious plight
When anti-Catholic riots broke out
Within the capital and thereabout.
He'd have to take a stand, without a doubt,
And meet the Dutch imposter face to face.

He made arrangements (hardly a disgrace –
A safe and sane precaution) to remove
The Queen and baby Prince to France. This move
Met with success. Mother and son set sail
From Portsmouth. James was resolved, without fail,
That his infant son and heir should survive,
Whatever his fate. Who would dare connive
Against the legitimate succession?
Quite a few, as it transpired. Possession
Of the name Stuart counted not a jot
For James Francis Edward – well, not a lot.

The King left London for Salisbury.
There his nerve deserted him. Treachery,
Alas, within the ranks of his army
Sapped his spirit. In the midlands, Derby
Declared for the Prince, then Nottingham too.
James swithered and dithered. What should he do?
The Earl of Danby took control of York,
Proof (once again) that he wasn't all talk.

Most of the north was for Orange, it seemed.
As his surly subjects plotted and schemed,
The King suffered a collapse. A martyr
To nosebleeds, battle was a non-starter.
He withdrew to his room for hours on end,
Nursing his hooter. His most sure friend
Deserted: John Churchill, his *protégé*,
His sworn brother-in-arms in exile, nay,
His page (at the tender age of sixteen),
His age-old chum and confidant. Obscene.

Rhyming History

William keeps his cool

James turned tail. With only one end in sight
He was now resolved, determined on flight.
Had he changed his mind and opted to fight,
The odds are he would have been trounced. And yet,
He'd have won some compassion – you bet!
William, you'll recall, was adamant
That he didn't come for the crown. Pure cant,
Of course, but poor James, by fleeing the land,
Strengthened the Prince's already strong hand.

Negotiation would have been far worse
For William. It might have seemed perverse
To meet his stricken uncle face to face
And quibble over terms. Will knew his place:
Watch and wait. The throne was the King's to lose.
The Prince kept his cool. He would let James choose.

James the Second, the Forgotten King

A daughter's betrayal

A further blow to the King's confidence
Was a bitter family circumstance.
Upon his return to London James found
That his younger daughter had gone to ground.

Princess Anne, Protestant, plain and stolid,
Was constant in her faith and rock solid
Against the Catholic threat (as perceived).
Her poor father was not a little peeved
At his daughter's defection, the final straw.
"My own children have forsaken me!" Oh, lor!

James moved to seek the advice of his peers
As to what he should do next. It appears
That he was prepared to negotiate –
He gave that impression at any rate.
He was urged to offer free elections
And to overlook the 'imperfections'
Of his rebellious Lords – to forgive,
In fact, all such renegades. As I live,
This was a tall order. The King thought ill
Of pardoning the likes of John Churchill.
It stuck in his throat and I'm not surprised.

But James was smarter than some realised.
He gave ground, and despatched Lords Godolphin,
Nottingham and Halifax (the linchpin)
To thrash out some semblance of an accord
With the Prince. He foresaw only discord,
However, in this enforced strategy.

Was he, the King, to be at the mercy
Of a 'free' Parliament? Was he heck!
Reduced though he was to a nervous wreck,

Rhyming History

James still had his pride. He told his cronies –
Catholic converts and other phonies –
That he was resolved to follow the Queen
Into exile. He wasn't quite so green
As to expect the rebels to play fair.
The King refused to be deposed, so there!

Richard the Second? Charles the First? No way!
King James would live to fight another day.

James' flight

Quite how, or where, is not for me to say,
Though exile proved to be no holiday –
Chez cousin Louis. Be that as it may,
James and his wee posse prepared for flight.
They made their escape in the dead of night,
Leaving mayhem and chaos in their wake.

William was invited, for the sake
Of peace and civil order, to take charge.
With rabid anti-papist mobs at large,
The Prince was the only choice within reach –
And thrilled he was to step into the breach.
Orange was always a fortunate chap.
It's as if the crown dropped into his lap.

But Lady Fortune was taking a nap
When the King in flight, by some strange mishap,
Was unexpectedly apprehended –
Not what the desperate James intended,
Nor the Prince, come to that. Around midnight
On the 10th of December, by moonlight,
He slipped down the back stairs out of Whitehall
With two trusted chums (not nervous at all)
And took a boat down the Thames to Vauxhall.

James the Second, the Forgotten King

Throwing caution to the winds, the Great Seal
He dropped into the water. This, I feel,
Epitomises the absurdity –
I'm tempted to say the perversity –
Of the King's sad state. His mood was hopeless.
As for his kingdom he couldn't care less.

His realm was in ruins, London on fire.
Why James is a figure some still admire
Is hard to credit. Hastening away,
They rode through the night and by break of day
Reached the Isle of Sheppey. It was there, by chance,
Upon boarding the boat to take them to France,
That one of their number was recognised.
The man was a local and much despised.

The King himself was heavily disguised –
But all three runaways were in for it.
Their captors took James for a Jesuit
And frisked the prisoners as they thought fit.
They searched the King "even to his privities" –
Sorry to offend your sensitivities.

Rhyming History

Welcome back to the King!

James, after sundry such indignities,
Was returned to London. A change of shirt,
A wash and a shave (removal of dirt
Is often a good tonic) and the King
Was much revived. Indeed, he felt something
Like his own self again. To some surprise,
He was warmly welcomed, cheered to the skies
In the Strand by his subjects, in whose eyes
A King, in triumph, was better by far
Than civil chaos. How fickle folk are.

One minute William's the rising star,
The next, their fugitive monarch – bizarre.

James, according to our friend John Evelyn,
Attended Mass and (into the bargain)
Dined in public. A Jesuit said grace –
Had James learnt nothing? Was he saving face,
Nothing more? He was still intent on flight.

His return, owing to an oversight
By William's messenger (who had failed
To tell the King to stay in Kent), derailed
The Prince's strategy. What should he do
With his errant uncle? Options were few.

To meet him face to face (this much he knew)
Were fatal. To be seen to drive James out,
Though, were worse by far, no shadow of doubt.
Tories were fundamentally loyal
To their monarch. James was the true royal.
A usurper would be hard to forgive –
A perilous precedent, as I live.
Something, or someone, would soon have to give.

James the Second, the Forgotten King

Touch and go for William

William had arrived by invitation.
This new, uncomfortable situation
Might encourage the political nation
(The Tories, at least) to turn again to their King,
A prospect, for the Prince, that was frightening.
Whatever Whigs might feel, however sickening,
The pace and danger of events was quickening.
The King was in London. Prince William was not.
This was about as precarious as it got.

Will was prepared to give it his best shot.
Tories could be a cantankerous lot.
He was careful to steer a middle path.
He didn't seek the throne (don't make me laugh),
But only came to serve the interest
Of freedom. Will continued to be blessed
By circumstance. Had the King decided
To stay put, far from being one-sided,
The struggle would have been messy at best.
However, in the event: no contest.

James for his own safety (no, I don't jest)
Was commanded to leave London for Ham,
Near Richmond in Surrey. Meek as a lamb,
The King requested to be sent instead
To Rochester in Kent. He made his bed...
Sniffing an advantage, the Prince agreed,
Willing a second escape to succeed.
The soldiers who guarded James were Dutch.
If he'd care to escape... Thanks very much!
William ordered that the King's back door
Should be left unattended. James forbore
To thank his subjects. Rather (very dim),
He blamed the people for forsaking him.

Escape to France

With the Duke of Berwick, his bastard son,
He stole away by night. The deed was done.
They took a rowing boat down the Medway,
Then a ship to France. Now an *émigré*,
The King landed *en France* on Christmas Day.

Dashed hopes and decrepitude, sad to say,
Were old James' destiny, death and decay.

The Prince of Orange was victorious –
His 'Revolution' dubbed 'Glorious'.
Courageous, resolute and strong-willed,
Was William's early promise fulfilled?

We shall see. His military campaigns,
Alas, led to few significant gains.
His was a disappointing legacy,
All said and done. The Stuart dynasty
Died out with Queen Anne. Hers was the glory –
But that, as they say, is another story.

Bibliography

Maurice Ashley, *England in the Seventeenth Century* (Penguin, 3rd ed. 1961)

John Bowle (ed.), *The Diary of John Evelyn* (Oxford University Press, 1983)

Barry Coward, *The Stuart Age. England, 1603-1714* (Pearson Education, 3rd ed. 2003)

Gila Curtis, *The Life and Times of Queen Anne* (Weidenfeld & Nicolson, with Book Club Associates, 1972)

Peter Earle, *The Life and Times of James II* (Weidenfeld & Nicolson, with Book Club Associates, 1972)

Charles George, *The Stuarts. A Century of Experiment, 1603-1714* (Hart-Davis Educational, 1975)

C. P. Hill, *Who's Who in Stuart Britain* (Shepheard-Walwyn, 1988)

John Miller, *James II* (Yale University Press, 2000)

John Miller, *The Life and Times of William and Mary* (Weidenfeld & Nicolson, with Book Club Associates, 1974)

John Miller, *The Stuarts* (Hambledon, 2006)

John Morrill, *The Stuarts* (in *The Oxford History of Britain,* ed. Kenneth O. Morgan – Oxford University Press, 2001)

Stuart Sim (ed.), *The Concise Pepys* (Wordsworth, 1997)

G. M. Trevelyan, *A Shortened History of England* (Penguin, 1959)